Making Sense of Sound

The Basics of Audio Electronics and Technology

Alvis J. Evans

PROMPT.
PUBLICATIONS

An Imprint of
Howard W. Sams & Company
Indianapolis, Indiana

REVISED FIRST EDITION, 1992

PROMPT® Publications is an imprint of Howard W. Sams & Company,
2647 Waterfront Parkway, East Drive, Indianapolis, IN 46214-2041.

This book was originally developed and then published as _The Electronics of Sound_ by:

    Master Publishing, Inc.
    14 Canyon Creek Village MS31
    Richardson, Texas 75080
    (214) 907-8938

International Standard Book Number: 0-7906-1026-4

Edited by: Charles Battle
Text Design and Artwork by: _Plunk Design, Dallas, TX_
Cover Design by: _Sara Wright_

Acknowledgements
All photographs not credited are either courtesy of Author, Master Publishing, Inc., or Howard W. Sams & Company.

Printed in the United States of America

9 8 7 6 5 4 3 2 1

TABLE OF CONTENTS

PREFACE

Have you ever wondered how sound is propagated, and how electronic techniques are used to sense and reproduce sound? Do you know what pitch is, or fidelity; or the lack of fidelity due to distortion? Have you ever wondered how sound is amplified to a level that produces pain, and why or why not the signal remains "distortionless." Do you know terms like noise figure, signal-to-noise ratio, filters, compression and expansion, heterodyning, Bode plots and transfer curves? Have you wondered how a cassette tape deck records and plays back signals, how tone controls work, what a phase-locked loop is, and how MTS TV works to produce stereo sound?

Making Sense of Sound was written to answer these questions and many more. It deals with the subject of sound—how it is detected and processed using electronics in equipment that spans the full spectrum of consumer electronics. *Making Sense of Sound* concentrates on explaining basic concepts and fundamentals to provide easy-to-understand information, yet it contains enough detail to be of high interest to the serious practitioner.

Making Sense of Sound begins by explaining sound, how sound propagates, and details sound's characteristics, e.g., pitch, loudness, phase, frequency spectrum, and quality characteristics of timbre, fidelity, distortion and noise. It discusses amplification principles and characteristics, and clarifies the difference between various types of amplifiers. It devotes a separate chapter to distortion and another to noise.

The chapter on distortion uses transfer curves to clearly illustrate how distortion occurs in amplifiers. The one on noise defines noise sources and explains noise figure and signal-to-noise ratio.

The chapters on sound transducers, AM/FM tuners and receivers, and video and TV stereo cover the full spectrum of equipment for producing monaural and stereo sound, including a detailed discussion of digital audio techniques. Interleaved within this group is a chapter on new sound concepts covering equalizers, compression and expansion, reverberation and echo, and music synthesizers.

Making Sense of Sound was designed to cover a broad scope, yet in enough detail to be a useful reference for student, technician, consumer and the experienced audiophile. We hope we have succeeded in that task.

A.J.E.

1

FUNDAMENTALS OF STEREO SOUND SYSTEMS

NATURE OF SOUND—WHAT IS IT?

Physiologically, sound is the sensation produced when the proper disturbance comes to the ear. In this sense, there are three requirements: (1) a source of sound, (2) a medium for transmitting the sound, and (3) an ear to detect the sound.

In the physical sense, sound is the stimulus capable of producing the sensation of sound. The stimulus is a series of disturbances in a medium which an ear interprets as sound. The disturbance may be thought of as a wave of pressure alternating above and below the equilibrium pressure in the medium. Though sound is usually transmitted through air, the medium of transmission may be solid, liquid, or gas. For example, if you were underwater when someone struck two rocks together in the water, you could hear the sound of the colliding rocks.

What does it take to produce a sound? Suppose we take a thin strip of hardwood or steel, like a popsicle stick or a hacksaw blade, and clamp one end tightly in a vise, as shown in *Figure 1-1*. If we pluck the free end of the strip, it produces a humming sound that we can hear. The molecules of the air transmit the disturbance or vibration by creating an alternating pressure wave of compressed and rarified air that propagates away from the strip, also shown in *Figure 1-1*. That is, the air molecules oscillate back and forth along the path in which the sound is traveling. Notice that the air molecules move only a short distance back and forth about or from their initial positions; they do not move away from the vibrating strip, but the wave does. A wave such as this, where the vibration of the individual particles is parallel to the direction that the wave travels, is called a *longitudinal wave*. *Figure 1-1* also shows that the position of the vibrating strip plotted against time produces a waveform called a *sine wave*. Eventually the amplitude A shown in *Figure 1-1* would reduce to zero as the energy provided to the strip is used up and the strip no longer vibrates.

Speed of Sound

Sound travels very fast, but its speed is not infinite and it is much slower than the speed of light. We can tell that it takes some time because we can see a distant lightning flash several seconds before we hear the resultant thunder. We also can hear echoes, which is sound reflecting from distant walls. The speed of sound varies with the medium temperature and the medium density. Generally, as the tempera-

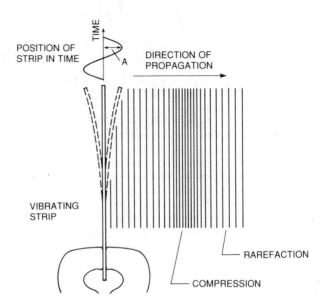

POSITION OF
STRIP IN TIME

TIME

A

DIRECTION OF
PROPAGATION

VIBRATING
STRIP

RAREFACTION

COMPRESSION

A thin strip clamped in a vise and made to vibrate produces a humming sound by causing
the air molecules to vibrate. Notice that the vibrating air particles constitute a longitudinal
wave while the position of the strip plotted against time is a transverse wave.

Figure 1-1. Sound wave propagation.

ture of the medium increases, the speed of sound increases. The rate at which the
speed increases in air is about 1.1 feet/second for each degree Fahrenheit.

The speed of sound in air is 1087 feet/second at 32 degrees Fahrenheit at sea
level. The speed of sound in water, which is denser than air, is about four times that
in air, or about 4757 feet/second. In some solids, the speed of sound is much
greater. In a steel rod, for example, the speed may be 16,500 feet/second, which is
about 15 times that in air. Because the speed of sound is finite and can be determined
for different mediums, it can be used to make some practical measurements. For
example, the thickness of material can be determined using sonar or ultrasonic
energy.

CHARACTERISTICS OF SOUND

Sounds differ from each other in several basic physical properties, each of which
has acoustic characteristics. The human ear is able to distinguish between two or
more sounds when the sounds differ in one or more of the characteristics of pitch,
loudness, or quality.

Pitch

Pitch is primarily associated with frequency; that is, the number of vibrations per second. Frequency is represented by f in equations and the unit of frequency is hertz (Hz). The period of the wave is the time (T) required for a single cycle of the wave to pass a given point. T is the reciprocal of f and vice versa:

$$T = \frac{1}{f}$$

T is in seconds

f is in Hertz (cycles per second)

$$f = \frac{1}{T}$$

Loudness

Loudness relates to the amplitude (A), or the intensity at which the energy is transmitted to the ear. The amplitude of wave motion, which is the maximum displacement of the vibrating particles of the medium, is determined by the amount of energy in the wave. The characteristics of frequency, period and amplitude (intensity) are illustrated in *Figure 1-2a*.

Quality

Quality, or *timbre*, refers to the complexity of the wave. It is illustrated in *Figure 1-2b*. When a sound is other than a pure sine wave of a single frequency, it is made up of a combination of sounds of more than one frequency. Timbre gives a sound a particular identity. It helps us distinguish one voice from another, or one musical instrument from another.

Audio Spectrum

Not all sound waves are capable of exciting the sensation of hearing. Infrasonic waves are so low in frequency that even though no sensation of sound is produced, pressure from the sound waves can be felt. On the other end of the audio frequency spectrum are ultrasonic waves, which are so high in frequency that no sensation of sound is produced in the human ear. We know these waves exist because it is possible to detect them by means other than the human ear. The extended audio spectrum showing the frequency range of various musical instruments is shown in *Figure 1-3*.

Phase

Two waves can be identical in frequency and amplitude, but can have a different *phase*. The waves can be in phase or can be out of phase by various amounts. If they are not exactly in phase, the amount of difference is called *phase shift*. It is a relative measure, related only to the particular waves being examined. Phase shift is often measured in degrees because the polar mathematical definition of a sine wave as it completes one cycle or period requires an amplitude vector A to rotate through 360 degrees.

When two waves A and B are combined, the resultant wave depends on their phase relation, their amplitudes, and their frequencies. A new wave results from constructive and destructive interference as indicated in *Figure 1-4*. When waves A and B have the same frequency and they are exactly in phase (*Figure 1-4c*), all parts add. When A and B are exactly 180 degrees out of phase, all parts subtract, and if

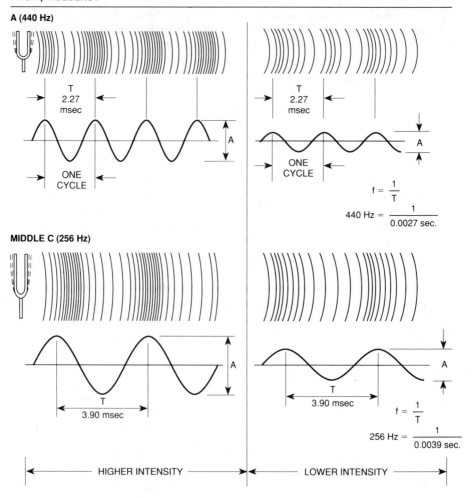

a. Pitch or Frequency is the Number of Vibrations Per Second. Intensity or Amplitude is the Amount of Energy Contained in the Wave.

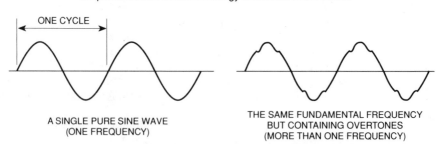

A SINGLE PURE SINE WAVE
(ONE FREQUENCY)

THE SAME FUNDAMENTAL FREQUENCY
BUT CONTAINING OVERTONES
(MORE THAN ONE FREQUENCY)

b. Timbre or Quality is the Purity of the Wave.

Figure 1-2. Characteristics of sound.

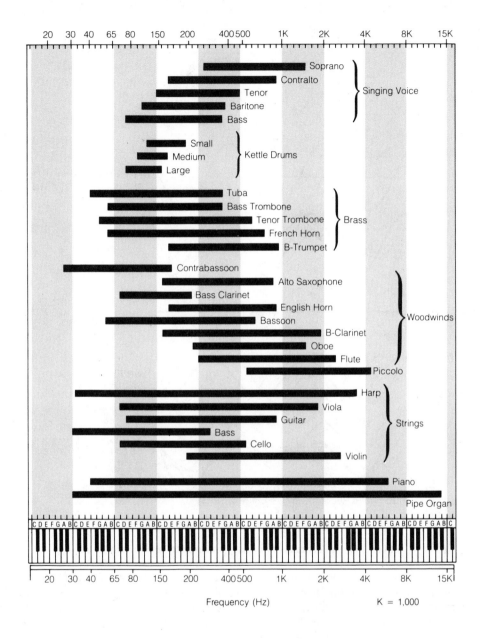

The range of human hearing extends from about 10 Hz to 20 kHz. The human voice and musical instruments fall within this range. Note than many instruments, particularly the string variety, span a wide range, and require a sound system that accurately reproduces these frequencies.

Figure 1-3. The audio spectrum showing various instruments and their range.

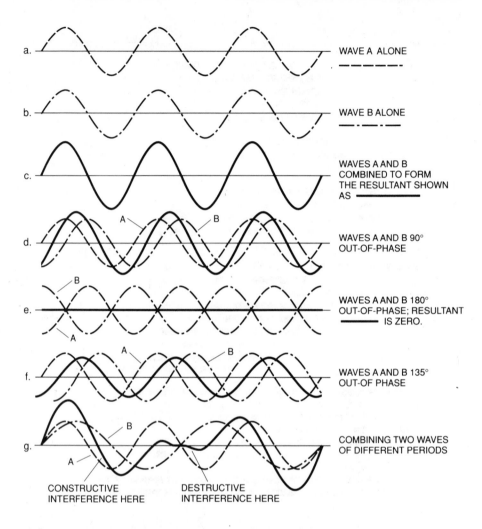

a.	WAVE A ALONE
b.	WAVE B ALONE
c.	WAVES A AND B COMBINED TO FORM THE RESULTANT SHOWN AS
d.	WAVES A AND B 90° OUT-OF-PHASE
e.	WAVES A AND B 180° OUT-OF-PHASE; RESULTANT IS ZERO.
f.	WAVES A AND B 135° OUT-OF PHASE
g.	COMBINING TWO WAVES OF DIFFERENT PERIODS

CONSTRUCTIVE INTERFERENCE HERE   DESTRUCTIVE INTERFERENCE HERE

Figure 1-4. The concepts of phase, phase shift, and interference.

the two waves are identical in amplitude and frequency (*Figure 1-4e*), the result is zero amplitude. Resultant waves when the phase relation of the equal frequency waves is 90° or 135° are shown in *Figures 1-4d* and *1-4f*, respectively. The resultant waveform when two waves of different frequencies are combined is shown in *Figure 1-4g*.

Wavelength

There is a simple relationship between the velocity (v in feet/second) of a wave, its frequency (f in Hz) and the distance (λ in feet) the wave travels in the time (T in seconds) of one complete vibration. This distance is called the *wavelength*. This relationship can be expressed by the following equation:

$$v = \frac{\lambda}{T}$$

and since
$$f = \frac{1}{T}$$

$\therefore$
$$v = \lambda f$$

and
$$\lambda = \frac{v}{f}$$

For example, if $v = 1100$ feet/second, then a 1100 Hz wave has a wavelength of one foot. It travels one foot while it completes one cycle, or one alternation of pressure.

Details of Characteristics

Intensity and Loudness

Intensity of sound is the rate at which the energy flows through a unit area. Since the *rate* at which energy flows is called *power*, sound intensity has the dimension of power per unit area (watts/square foot or watts/square centimeter). While some waves do not transmit sufficient energy to excite the sensation of hearing, others transmit too much energy and the sensation becomes one of pain. As shown in *Figure 1-5*, however, the human ear can accommodate a very great *amplitude dynamic range*. That is, the threshold of pain at 10^{-4} watt/sq. cm. is 1,000,000,000,000 (a thousand billion) times louder than the threshold of hearing at 10^{-16} watt/sq. cm. For convenience in expressing sound intensities with this extreme range, we use the decibel (dB) when dealing with sound levels. Notice in *Figure 1-5* that 0 dB SPL corresponds to the threshold of hearing. (See Appendix for a discussion of the decibel.)

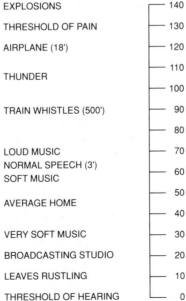

EXPLOSIONS	140
THRESHOLD OF PAIN	130
AIRPLANE (18')	120
	110
THUNDER	
	100
TRAIN WHISTLES (500')	90
	80
LOUD MUSIC	70
NORMAL SPEECH (3')	
SOFT MUSIC	60
	50
AVERAGE HOME	
	40
VERY SOFT MUSIC	30
BROADCASTING STUDIO	20
LEAVES RUSTLING	10
THRESHOLD OF HEARING	0

SOUND PRESSURE LEVEL (SPL) IN DECIBELS (dB)

Figure 1-5. The intensity levels of certain sounds.

The *loudness* of a sound is the amplitude of the auditory sensation produced by the sound and is related to the intensity. Generally sound waves of higher intensity are louder; however, the ear is not equally sensitive to sounds of all frequencies. Consequently, a sound of one frequency may seem louder than one of another frequency having the same intensity. *Figure 1-6* shows this relationship between the limits of audibility, intensity and frequency for a person with average hearing ability.

The measurement of loudness is important for practical purposes. This measurement, however, is difficult to achieve because the perception of loudness varies between individuals and depends on frequency, phase and timbre. Intensity, on the other hand, is measured with acoustical apparatus and does not depend on the hearing ability of the observer.

The sensation of hearing S, or *sound level*, is proportional to the logarithm of the intensity I:

$$S = \log \frac{I}{I_o} \quad \text{or} \quad 10^S = \frac{I}{I_o}$$

(See Appendix for a brief review of logarithms.) If the actual sound intensity, I, is 10 times greater than the reference intensity, I_o, then S has increased by one unit. The zero reference of sound level is chosen to be an intensity I_o that corresponds to the threshold of human hearing and is the lowest *sound pressure level* (SPL) that the average ear can perceive. This is equal to 0 dB SPL.

Sound pressure levels and intensity levels are normally expressed in decibels (dB). A decibel is the logarithm of a non-dimensional ratio of two power-like quantities. For two power levels, P_1 and P_2, P_2 can be expressed in dB relative to P_1 by:

$$dB = 10 \log \frac{P_2}{P_1}$$

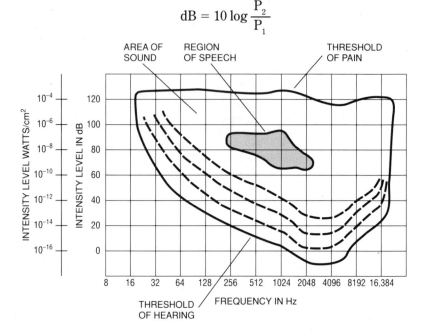

Figure 1-6. The limits of a person with average hearing.

Sound pressure levels (SPLs) are related to intensity in that intensity is a power per unit area, and 0 dB SPL is an intensity of, I_o, of 10^{-16} watts/cm^2 or 10^{-12} watts/m^2. As a result, the difference in intensity, I and I_o, can be expressed in dB as:

$$dB = 10 \log_{10} \frac{I}{I_o}$$

Sound waves are disbursed in all directions from a vibrating source. If the medium is uniform, they spread out in a spherical pattern as seen in *Figure 1-7*. The area of the expanding wave front is proportional to the square of the distance from the source and the *total power* is constant. Thus, the intensity of the wave diminishes as it moves away from the source. A sound wave 20 feet from its source is one-fourth as intense as it is 10 feet from the source. At 40 feet, the intensity is 1/16 of that at 10 feet.

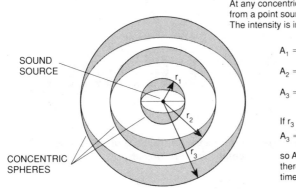

At any concentric spherical surface, the energy from a point source is spread over a area $4\pi r^2$. The intensity is inversely proportional to this area.

SOUND SOURCE

CONCENTRIC SPHERES

$A_1 = 4\pi r_1^2$

$A_2 = 4\pi r_2^2$

$A_3 = 4\pi r_3^2$

If r_3 is $3r_1$, then:
$A_3 = 4\pi(3r_1)^2 = 4\pi 9 r_1^2$

so A_3 is 9 times as great as A_1; therefore, intensity at A_3 surface is 9 times less than at A_1.

Figure 1-7. In a uniform medium, sound travels in a spherical pattern from its source, causing intensity to vary inversely with area (square of distance).

Tone Quality or Timbre

The simplest form of periodic motion, as illustrated in *Figure 1-1*, is the sine wave. The unique thing about a sine wave is that it exists as a single pure frequency called a *fundamental*. Whole number multiples of the fundamental are called harmonics or overtones. A note of a given pitch sounded on the piano is easily distinguished from one of the same pitch sounded, for example, on the clarinet. The difference in the two tones is called *tone quality* or *timbre* and depends on the number of harmonics present and their amplitude relative to the amplitude of the fundamental. *Figure 1-8* shows the waveforms and relative amplitude of the frequency compo- nents in three different kinds of musical instruments—tuning fork, piano and clarinet when playing a C.

This concept is summarized in the Fourier (pronounced F'au-re-ay) theorem which says that all waveforms other than the sine wave are complex, and are comprised of a fundamental frequency and a series of harmonically related frequen- cies. The basic composition of complex waveforms is shown in *Figure 1-9*. The proper combination of the single fundamental sine wave with its harmonics produces a sound that is richer and fuller; that is, the tone quality is improved.

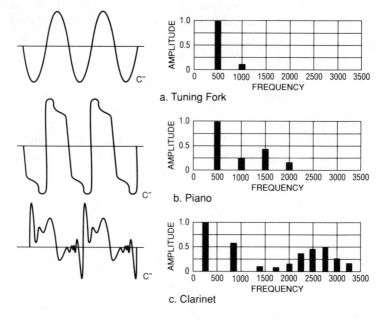

a. Tuning Fork

b. Piano

c. Clarinet

Figure 1-8. Waveforms and frequency distributions of tones produced by different musical instruments.

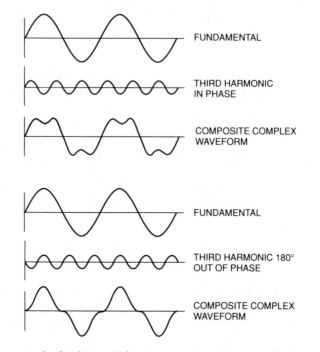

FUNDAMENTAL

THIRD HARMONIC
IN PHASE

COMPOSITE COMPLEX
WAVEFORM

FUNDAMENTAL

THIRD HARMONIC 180°
OUT OF PHASE

COMPOSITE COMPLEX
WAVEFORM

Figure 1-9. The fundamental frequency and complex waveforms composed of harmonically related sine waves.

Quality Features of Sound—Fidelity, Distortion, Noise

The best sound reproduction is that which offers the listener, as nearly as possible, an exact replica of the original sound. *Fidelity* is the term that describes the amount of trueness a reproduced sound has compared to the original sound. A *distortion* is any difference between the original and the reproduced sound. It may take various forms, such as frequency distortion or harmonic distortion. We will discuss distortion in detail in Chapter 3. The term *high fidelity* refers to sound reproduction in which the various distortions are kept so low that most listeners cannot detect them.

Noise in a sound system is any undesired disturbance which distracts from the clean, clear tones of music, speech or other audio signals. As commonly understood, noise is audible, although in a wider sense it also covers visual disturbances such as "snow" occurring in television reception. The common classes of noise are: (1) *static*, which may be caused by a poor connection of a plug, jack, or solder joint; (2) *hum*, possibly from a defective power supply or induced into audio cables from nearby electrical lines; and (3) *hiss*, which can be emitted from a carbon composition resistor or the playback from a tape-recorded signal. We will discuss the causes and cures of noise in Chapter 7.

TYPICAL STEREO SYSTEM COMPONENTS

Modern stereo systems usually contain at least three basic equipment sections: a signal source, an amplifier and a speaker system. *Figure 1-10a* shows the basic sections and *Figure 1-10b* shows the individual components of a typical stereo system. Most audiophiles (high-fidelity purists) prefer component systems over console systems. Detailed specifications for each separate component help them determine the overall system performance when their chosen components are connected together. Because component input and output levels, impedances, and connectors have been standardized by manufacturers, components from different manufacturers can be intermixed and connected with audio cables to form the complete system. We will now discuss the individual components.

Signal Sources

Turntables or Record Changers

An entire home entertainment industry was born in 1876 when Thomas Edison invented the phonograph. It uses the principle of a needle moving back and forth to follow record grooves to produce mechanical motion which is converted into electrical signals. The phonograph enjoyed dominance as a signal source until the 1980s, when it was replaced by the cassette tape, and later the compact disc (CD).

Tape Systems

Tape systems, including tape recorders, players and decks, are a standard part of a typical stereo system. A tape system can have a reel-to-reel, cartridge or cassette format. Cassette systems are most popular because of convenience, small size, low cost, high reliability and high-quality performance.

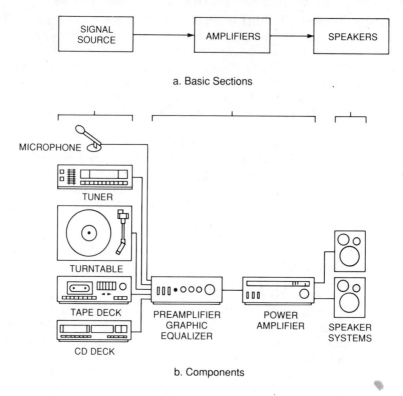

a. Basic Sections

b. Components

Figure 1-10. Modern stereo systems

Compact Disc

The compact disc is the sound reproduction system designed to replace the phonograph LP as the dominant playback medium in the home stereo system. CD players also are being used in automobiles and small portable systems that can operate while being carried. It combines several revolutionary and evolutionary technological processes in its design, such as optical scanning, digital signal sampling, processing and storage, and error detection and correction circuitry. As remarkable as the CD system is, it is the infant pioneer in the digital domain of sound recording and reproduction.

AM/FM Tuners

The convenience of having an almost endless supply of music and other program material without the expense and handling of records, cassette tapes, or CDs make the AM/FM tuner a very popular audio signal source.

FM (Frequency Modulation) differs from AM (Amplitude Modulation) in both the method of signal transmission and the quality of the audio signal produced. FM signals have a wider bandwidth and can be processed to remove static and noise interference, which are primarily AM by nature. The result is an audio signal that is higher in fidelity and lower in noise than AM. Stereo reproduction has been a common part of FM for about three decades, but it is a relatively new feature of AM.

Microphones

Technically, a microphone is an electroacoustical transducer that converts sound waves (changes in air pressure) into electrical signals. Several varieties exist and are classified according to their basic principle of operation and the way they pick up sounds.

Amplifiers

The amplifier is needed because the signals from most sources are too weak to operate a speaker directly. Amplifiers are often separated into preamplifiers and power amplifiers. Whether connected as separate components or combined into one integrated component, they form the heart of every stereo sound system.

Preamplifiers

The preamplifier is a small-signal voltage amplifier that increases the amplitude of the signal source output. In addition, it has circuits which equalize auxiliary input signal sources for overall flat frequency response. It also has jacks, switches and other controls so it can serve as an audio control center. The control center function of the preamplifier allows the user to select the signal source and to adjust volume, loudness, tone (bass to treble equalization) and channel balance for improving the overall sound performance. Other filters and controls may be included to correct for noise, differences in hearing, room resonances, or speaker placement.

Power Amplifiers

Alternating voltage alone is insufficient to drive the speakers and produce audio power. There must be enough current as well as voltage for adequate power. The amount of power is given by the equation:

$$P = I \times E$$

where P is in watts, I is in amperes, and E is in volts. I and E are the effective values of the alternating current and voltage, respectively. They are assumed to be in phase because the speaker is assumed to be a resistive load.

The requirements of a power amplifier are: flat frequency response, low noise, low distortion, stability with temperature and load variations, and sufficient power output to operate the speakers.

Integrated Amplifier-Receiver

Because most of the components of a modern stereo system contain integrated circuits (ICs), the components can be housed in small cases. Usually the operator controls and mechanical components dictate the case size. Designers can pack a preamplifier, power amplifier, AM/FM tuner, and a tape deck or CD player into one integrated package, which some people prefer.

Speakers

The final sound and ultimate performance of the stereo sound system depends upon the performance of the speakers. A speaker system converts the electric signal from the power amplifier to mechanical motion which produces sound waves which can be heard. The term "speaker" usually refers to more than the actual speaker itself. It also refers to an enclosure with one or more drivers. The sound produced by the speaker system depends upon its specifications, of which power rating, efficiency, and frequency response are most important. To learn more about speakers, see *Speakers for Your Home and Automobile,* by Gordon McComb, published by Howard W. Sams & Company.

Cables and Connectors

Cables, connectors, plugs, and jacks are the cause of many stereo system problems. Using the correct cable impedance and length are important for good frequency response and low noise. The connector or cable is frequently damaged or the solder connection broken by use or abuse where the cable bends at the connector.

Most connecting cables of 25 feet or less are unbalanced line types which have an insulated single center conductor with a braided metal shield around it as shown in *Figure 1-11a.* The shield is usually connected to the system ground so it protects the audio signal from noise interference. The cable shown in *Figure 1-11a* is called an unbalanced line cable because the signal conductor is at a different impedance from the shield which is at system common or ground. A balanced line cable, shown in *Figure 1-11b,* has two signal conductors inside the metal braided shield. This type of cable is called a balanced line because both signal paths (forward and return) are equal impedances from ground. Satisfactory audio cables of several hundred feet are possible by using the balanced line cable.

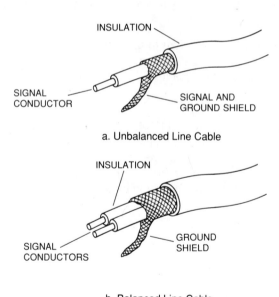

a. Unbalanced Line Cable

b. Balanced Line Cable

Figure 1-11. Cables

2

ABOUT
AMPLIFIERS

AMPLIFICATION PRINCIPLES

An *amplifier* is an electronic circuit which increases the amplitude of an electronic signal. It is one of the most important building blocks in a stereo system. Although various types of amplifiers are used in stereo systems, all of them perform the basic function of increasing the amplitude of the electronic signal.

Recall that a microphone converts acoustical energy into electrical energy. The electrical energy derived from microphones, as well as other sources, is generally very small—typically in microvolts (millionths of a volt) or millivolts (thousandths of a volt). These weak signals have to be *amplified* before they can be used effectively. For example, with suitable amplification, the signals drive the stereo system's speakers and we can hear an acceptable level of sound output. *Figure 2-1* shows some systems that use amplifiers.

How Amplification is Accomplished

An amplifier uses one or more semiconductor devices along with a number of associated components. Their combined purpose is to increase the strength of the applied signal. The semiconductor device is usually a bipolar junction transistor (BJT) or a field-effect transistor (FET); both of these are active devices which provide amplification. An *active device* is an electronic component capable of controlling current in a way that produces amplification (gain). The associated components are passive components such as resistors, capacitors, diodes, inductors and transformers. The passive components control the operation of the active devices and shape the amplifier's overall characteristics to the desired specifications.

In regard to amplifiers, the term *stage* usually refers to the circuitry consisting of an active device and its supporting associated components. It usually takes multiple stages to provide the total amplification required. It is one step in a multistep process.

Years ago almost all amplifiers used vacuum tubes as active devices, but today much of the circuitry in modern stereo amplifiers is on integrated circuit (IC) chips. Each IC can have a dozen or more external connections, and from dozens to thousands of components on the chip. Examples of semiconductor devices and integrated circuits used as audio amplifiers, as well as a vacuum tube, are shown in *Figure 2-2*.

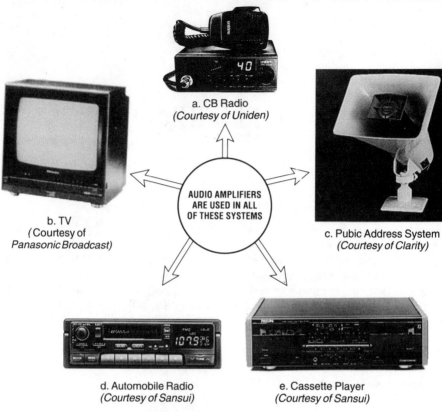

a. CB Radio
(Courtesy of Uniden)

b. TV
*(Courtesy of
Panasonic Broadcast)*

AUDIO AMPLIFIERS
ARE USED IN ALL
OF THESE SYSTEMS

c. Pubic Address System
(Courtesy of Clarity)

d. Automobile Radio
(Courtesy of Sansui)

e. Cassette Player
(Courtesy of Sansui)

Figure 2-1. Applications in which audio amplifiers are used.

RECTIFIER

VACUUM
TUBE

INTEGRATED
CIRCUITS

TRANSISTORS

Figure 2-2. Active components used in audio amplifers.
(Courtesy of Radio Shack)

The concept of how amplification is accomplished is shown in *Figure 2-3* with a generic active device depicted as a variable resistor. In order to amplify, the active device must be capable of producing a relatively large change in its output in response to a small change at its input. The resistance across the output terminals of the active device varies as the input signal varies. Therefore, the current supplied by the battery through the device and the load resistor changes. This current is the *output current*. Current changes through resistors cause voltage changes across the resistors. In this case, the voltage change across the device is based on the ratio of its resistance to the total resistance in the circuit.

The voltage across the device is the *output voltage*. If the input signal can cause the resistance across the output terminals of the active device to vary from the extremes of an open (infinite resistance) to a short (zero resistance), then the output current will vary from zero to some maximum value. This maximum value is determined by Ohm's law. In this case, it is 12 volts (the supply voltage) divided by the load resistance. Note that the large change in output current and output voltage is only *controlled* by the small input voltage, and that energy is not, and cannot, be created. Any increase in power to the output is supplied by the power supply.

Now, let's look at a basic amplifier using an actual active device in place of the generic device of *Figure 2-3*.

Basic Amplifier Stage

In *Figure 2-4*, each of three different types of active devices is shown in a simplified amplifier circuit. A sine wave is shown as the input and output signal. The electron path of prime importance is shown by the dotted line. Each circuit has two dc power supplies shown as battery cells. One of the supplies is for output power and one is for bias. *Bias* is the voltage or current that establishes the no-signal (quiescent) operating condition of the active device. In most practical amplifier circuits, a single dc power supply supplies both output power and bias.

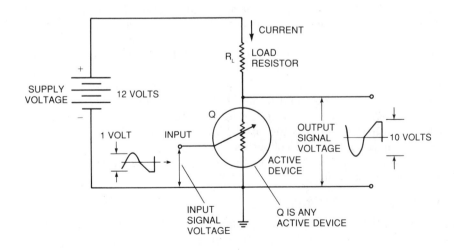

Figure 2-3. How amplification is accomplished using an active device.

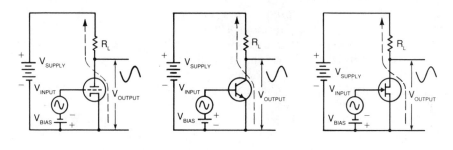

a. Vacuum Tube   b. Bipolar Junction Transistor   c. Field-Effect Transistor

Figure 2-4. Same basic amplifier using three different active devices.

Two popular bias arrangements for bipolar junction transistors are shown in *Figure 2-5*. The *fixed current bias* circuit, as shown in *Figure 2-5a*, is the simplest and requires the minimum number of components. However, this circuit is somewhat unstable and inflexible. The *voltage divider bias* using an emitter resistor, as shown in *Figure 2-5b*, is the most popular amplifier circuit using a bipolar junction transistor.

Voltage or Power

Voltage and power amplifiers are significantly different in both their function and operation. An audio voltage amplifier is an amplifier circuit that provides large changes in voltage amplitudes but operates at low current. It increases a low voltage input signal to the amplitude required at the input of a power amplifier. In contrast, an audio power amplifier must operate at high current levels to drive speakers to produce a substantial sound power level. Solid-state power amplifiers usually operate at low voltage; however, vacuum tube power amplifiers operate at high voltage and high current. The high power amplifier, providing from a few watts to several hundred watts, is the last stage of amplification before a signal leaves the amplifier chain to drive a speaker.

The devices used for power amplifiers, as well as their associated components, are required to dissipate significant power within themselves. Therefore, in addition to operating over a wide dynamic range of voltage *and* current, they must be capable of dissipating power in the form of heat. Remember that power is equal to voltage multiplied by current. Voltage can exist without current when impedance is infinite, but current, determined by the voltage and impedance that is present, cannot exist without voltage.

Input and Output Impedance

Impedance is the total opposition (resistance and reactance) a circuit or device offers to alternating current at a given frequency. Ideally, an amplifier should have infinite input impedance and zero output impedance. This would allow the amplifier to cause no current drain on the previous stage or its source and an unlimited ability

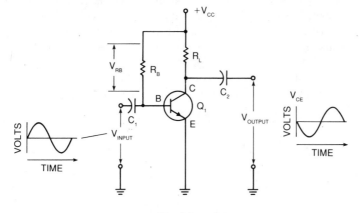

a. Fixed Current

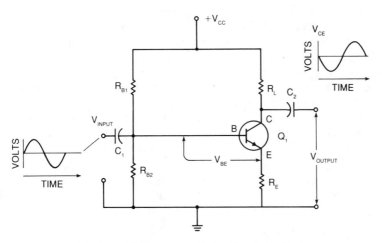

b. Voltage Divider with an Emitter Feedback Resistor

Figure 2-5. Bias circuit arrangements.

to drive the next stage. A typical *voltage amplifier*, however, has an output impedance of thousands of ohms. This high output impedance usually causes no real
problem because a small-signal voltage amplifier usually does not have to drive a
load (the input to the next stage) requiring a large current. A *power amplifier* should
always have a very low output impedance.

Discrete or Integrated

For at least four decades, electronics in sound applications utilized the vacuum tube
as its active element. The development of the transistor permitted denser packaging and smaller systems. Integrated circuits provide a means to incorporate all the
circuitry into solid-state material. Most modern stereo systems incorporate high-
density packaging in the form of linear and/or digital ICs.

Audio systems place some unique and stringent requirements upon IC parameters. The IC is called upon to process complex ac signals with frequencies ranging from 20 Hz to 20 kHz, with amplitudes varying from a few microvolts to several volts, and with a transient nature characterized by steep wavefronts separated by unknown periods of absolute silence. The processing must be done without adding any noise or distortion. As shown in *Figure 2-2*, active devices have evolved from the vacuum tube, through the transistor, to the integrated circuit.

PREAMPLIFIER – SMALL-SIGNAL OR VOLTAGE AMPLIFIERS

Functions of Preamplifiers

The primary purpose of a preamplifier is to increase the level of a low-level signal so it can be processed further without appreciable degradation in its quality. A preamplifier may also include provisions for equalizing, mixing, level control, balance control, and other controls. Preamplifiers are sometimes classified as *source preamplifiers* or *control preamplifiers*

A source preamplifier is often used in tape or compact disc decks immediately following the detector circuit of a tuner. It can even be within a microphone housing to increase the level of weak signals before they are transferred through audio cables. This makes the signals stronger than the noise picked up by the audio cables so the signals can override the noise.

A control preamplifier performs at least three functions: (1) it equalizes the source signal for overall flat frequency response, (2) it further amplifies the signal, and (3) it acts as a control center. Almost every part of a sound system is designed to have a flat frequency response for true sound reproduction, but the control preamplifier circuits can adjust the frequency response for improving the overall sound performance. The frequency response of the system can be changed to compensate for noise, and for differences in hearing, room acoustics, and speaker system characteristics. Control circuits have adjustments for loudness, volume, tone and channel balance. Let's look at each of these in more detail.

Loudness and Volume

At first glance, the loudness control and volume control appear to be the same. However, as we saw in *Figure 1-6*, the sensitivity of the human ear decreases at very low and high frequencies. The loudness control increases the strength of the low frequencies, and sometimes the high frequencies, at low listening levels so that the listener's perceived loudness of each frequency is the same as the loudness of a 1000 Hz tone.

A volume control is a voltage divider (usually a variable resistor) that adjusts the percentage of the signal without regard to frequency that is applied from one stage to the next. Decreasing the amplitude of a signal is called *attenuation* and the control that adjusts the attenuation is often called an *attenuator*. Some high performance sound systems may have step attenuators providing descrete intervals instead of continuously variable types.

Tone Controls

Manufacturers often omit loudness control circuits to reduce production costs. They rationalize that the same results can be obtained with the tone control circuits. While that is true, the effect is not automatic as it is with the loudness control.

Tone controls allow the user to adjust the amplifier frequency response of the bass, mid-range and treble frequency ranges to compensate for speaker response limitations and listening room acoustics, and to suit personal taste. The ultimate in tone control is the equalizer, which allows several small bands of frequencies to be individually attenuated or boosted.

Balance

A balance control is used in all stereo preamplifiers to correct for differences in sound volume between the left and right channels. There are several methods used to provide this volume balance. The simplest method, used on the very inexpensive stereos, is to use a concentric double-shaft volume control so each channel can be adjusted separately if desired. The two shafts are loosely interlocked by a light friction fit so both normally move together, though they can be adjusted separately by using two hands. More expensive stereos use a single control.

Two such circuits for balance control are shown in *Figure 2-6*. The circuit in *Figure 2-6a* is the simplest, though it produces a slight amount of crosstalk between the channels. It produces a signal insertion loss of 3 dB in both channels when the control is moved to the center. When moved to one end, one channel will be reduced to zero and the other channel will be 3 dB louder. The very common circuit shown in *Figure 2-6b* uses a ganged double-variable resistor which has almost no insertion loss at its full right or full left position. However, it has a 6 dB insertion loss at the center.

CONVENTIONAL POWER AMPLIFIERS

As its name implies, the audio power amplifier increases the power of an input audio signal. As mentioned previously, it differs from a voltage amplifier in that it operates at high current to deliver amplified power to its load. For this reason, power amplifiers are often referred to as current amplifiers.

In addition to the amplifier stages, some power amplifiers also incorporate circuits to protect the output stage devices and the speakers from high current overloads that are a result of short circuits or pulse signals generated by on-off switching. The power amplifier has five main stages as shown in the block diagram of *Figure 2-7*.

Input and Predriver

The first block in the power amplifier is the input stage, usually a low-level transistor or operational amplifier IC with high efficiency and low noise. The input stage is designed to operate as a buffer for increasing the input impedance of the power amplifier and to improve its stability. Because of the large amount of negative feedback, there is very little voltage gain in the input stage. Negative feedback is used to reduce distortion. Almost all of the voltage gain is produced in the predriver stage.

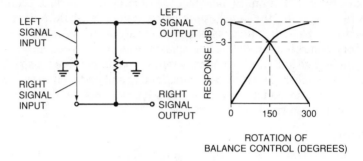

a. Single Variable Resistor

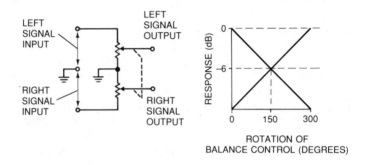

b. Ganged Variable Resistor

Figure 2-6. Balance controls.

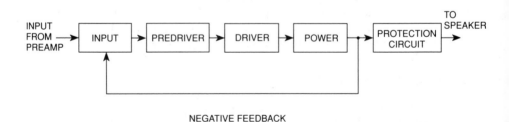

Figure 2-7. Five main stages of a power amplifier.

The Driver

The driver stage is a current amplifier that provides the driving current for the final power stage. Very high power amplifiers may have two cascaded driver stages to increase the signal power to a level sufficient to drive the final power amplifier to its rated maximum output.

Figure 2-8 shows a schematic diagram of a typical audio power amplifier similar to the driver and power blocks shown in *Figure 2-7*. The power active devices are inside the block marked IC201. Notice the diodes in the driver block. Since the transistors in the driver and power stages must handle large amounts of power, they normally generate substantial heat. The diodes correct any variations in performance caused by the changes in temperature of the transistors since the temperature characteristic of the diodes is similar to that of the transistors. Thermistors and varistors are also commonly used for temperature compensation and bias stabilization in place of the diodes.

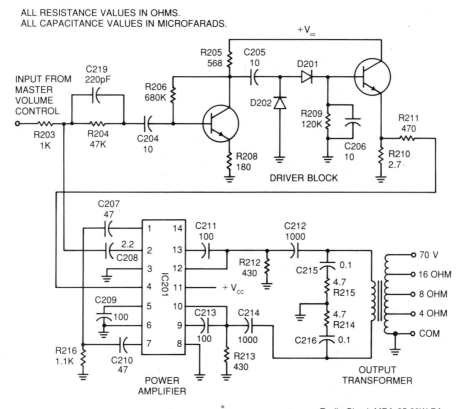

Figure 2-8. Typical audio amplifiers schematic.
(Courtesy of Radio Shack)

The Power Stage

Look at the circuit in *Figure 2-9.* In the A half of the input signal cycle, V_1 causes current in Q1 which drives transformer T2. Q2 is off. During the B half of the input signal cycle, V_2 causes current in Q2 which drives transformer T2. Q1 is off. Because Q1 and Q2 alternately drive T2 in each half of the cycle, the circuit is called a push-pull circuit.

By cutting the circuit in half as indicated by the dotted line in *Figure 2-9,* the circuit becomes a single-transistor power amplifier stage. However, it is not likely to be found in modern circuits because it requires a large iron-core transformer and a substantial continuous dc bias current, making it extremely heavy and inefficient.

Although the push-pull circuit requires a transformer, it is much more efficient. Resistors R1 and R2 set the bias current of the transistors to just slightly on rather than the heavy bias current of the single-transistor circuit. Because of the reduced dc bias current, there is less chance of magnetically saturating the transformer's iron core; therefore, a smaller, lighter and less expensive transformer can be used. The push-pull amplifier requires two identical complementary signals that are 180 degrees out of phase. These signals are V_1 and V_2 in *Figure 2-9.* They are supplied by the center-tapped secondary of input transformer T1.

The complementary signals also can be provided by a transistor phase splitter. The circuit looks similar to the circuit shown in *Figure 2-5b,* with an output signal taken from the emitter as well as the collector. The two signals are complementary signals 180 degrees out of phase. Such a circuit requires a coupling capacitor and R_L equal to R_E. Any time coupling capacitors are used in an amplifier, or any other network, the low-end frequency response is reduced. Also, if the power amplifier requires a very large driving current, then the idle current through the phase splitter Q_1 will have to be large, producing heat that has to be dissipated. One type of push-pull amplifier that does not require input or output transformers and, in fact, does not even require a phase splitter is the *complementary* amplifier.

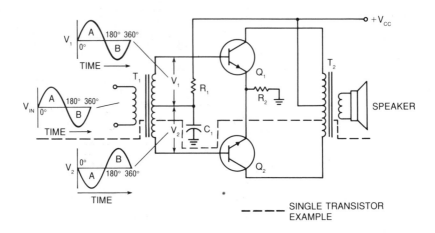

Figure 2-9. Push-pull audio amplifier using an output transformer.

Complementary Amplifiers

The complementary amplifier circuit of *Figure 2-10* uses a PNP type and a NPN type transistor. Except for polarity, the transistors have the same electrical characteristics. A positive voltage on the base (input) of the NPN transistor causes it to conduct. A negative voltage on the base of the PNP transistor causes it to conduct. The two emitters are connected together with resistors R6 and R7, and the two transistors are connected in series through their collectors across the power supply (between V_{cc} and ground). When the transistors are properly biased, the voltage at A will be one-half the voltage of the power supply because the circuit current will be balanced through each transistor. When a silicon transistor is properly biased, approximately 0.7 volt is between its base and emitter. This means that 1.4 volts should be between the bases of Q_2 and Q_3, which is maintained by diodes D_1 and D_2. During one-half of the input signal cycle, one transistor conducts; during the other half of the signal cycle, the other transistor conducts. This alternate push-pull conduction operation provides efficient, low-distortion, medium-power amplifier performance.

When large power output is needed, the basic complementary amplifier circuit may not produce enough power by itself because it becomes more difficult to match PNP and NPN at higher power ratings. Also, power PNP transistors cost more than their NPN counterpart. To obtain more power output, therefore, circuits have been devised to use only NPN large-power transistors. Such a circuit is shown in *Figure 2-11*.

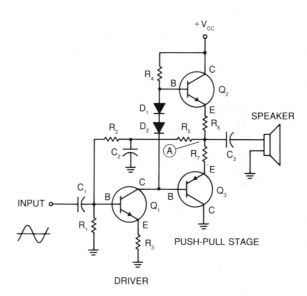

Figure 2-10. Complementary push-pull power amplifier with a single stage driver.

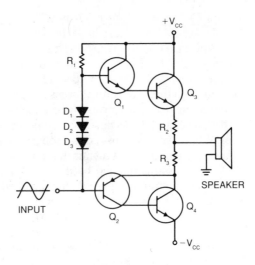

Figure 2-11. Quasi-complementary power amplifier stage.

Notice that the NPN transistors, Q_1 and Q_3 in *Figure 2-11,* are connected in a Darlington configuration. The PNP-NPN complementary pair, Q_2 and Q_4, also form a Darlington. A Darlington acts like a single high-gain transistor. This circuit is referred to as a *quasi-complementary* amplifier because it operates like a complementary amplifier, but it does not require complementary high-power output transistors. The three series-connected diodes provide a voltage drop that serves to thermally stabilize the transistors.

Coupling Between Stages and to the Speaker

Direct coupling between stages, and between the power amplifier output stage and the loudspeaker, improves the stability of the amplifier and removes the reactive effects (frequency and phase distortion) that would occur if coupling capacitors or transformers were used. The size, weight and expense of interstage or output transformers used in earlier amplifiers is unacceptable today. Therefore, they have been virtually eliminated in the modern audio amplifier.

The amplifier circuit of *Figure 2-9* uses an output transformer to couple to the speaker. The complementary amplifier of *Figure 2-10* couples the signal to the speaker from the amplifier output with a capacitor. Since the speaker input is at a higher voltage than ground, the transformer or the coupling capacitor is required to prevent DC through the speaker. The circuit of *Figure 2-11* eliminates the need for a coupling capacitor because the output circuit, with equal positive and negative supplies, produces zero dc voltage at the speaker. The speaker can be directly connected to the output circuit, therefore, it is called an *output capacitor-less* (OCL) amplifier.

Although direct coupling seems to be all good, there are some disadvantages. It is temperature sensitive and requires a well-regulated power supply. Some of these problems can be reduced by using a negative feedback system. When negative feedback is used, the amplifier will have good stability and will generally have a very flat low-frequency response.

When coupling an amplifier to a speaker, there is a factor called the amplifier's *damping factor*. The advertised damping factor is defined as the rated load divided by the amplifier's output impedance. A damping factor greater than 10 is adequate.

Protection Circuits

Protection circuits are used in the power supply, audio power amplifier, and the speaker system. These circuits prevent extensive and expensive damage if an overload or short circuit occurs. It is important to realize that *either* a short or an open of the amplifier output can damage the output transistors. Care should be taken when connecting or testing the speaker system to avoid an open or a short condition. An excessively high input signal can also cause a current over the rating of the power transistors and possibly destroy them. This over-current damage may be prevented with a fuse in the output circuit; however, a fuse protection system may be too slow to prevent damage if the overload is abrupt and intense.

Muting Circuit

If the power amplifier output is capacitor coupled to the speaker, a large pulse of capacitor charging current flows through the speaker when the main power switch is turned on. In addition to the annoying loud pop it causes, the current pulse may cause speaker damage. A muting circuit used in many systems delays the connection of the power supply voltage to the power amplifier until the output coupling capacitor has had time to charge. An alternate method delays connection of the amplifier to the speaker.

CLASSES OF AMPLIFIERS

Standard amplifier operation can be divided into various classes which are dependent upon the device operating point and the amplitude of the input signal. The device operating point is determined by the device's characteristics and the amount of bias on the device. These two factors primarily determine the length of time, or number of electrical degrees, that current will pass through the device during the application of a cycle of sinusoidal input signal. The classes into which amplifier operation is divided are Class A, Class B, Class C and some combinations of these three. *Figure 2-12* shows the waveforms associated with the various classes of operation.

Class A operation is defined as the selection of a bias point and an input signal value that will allow current through the device during the complete input cycle. With Class A operation, the distortion is low, the voltage amplification is high, and the power output and the efficiency are relatively low.

Class B operated amplifiers have the bias set near the cutoff point so when a sine wave input signal is applied, there is an output signal for approximately half a cycle. This is the mode used in the circuits of *Figure 2-9* through *2-11*.

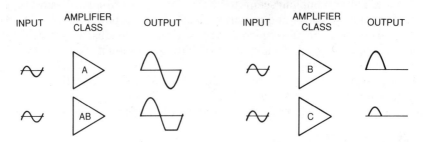

Figure 2-12. Class A, Class AB, Class B and Class C operation

In the Class AB amplifier, the operating bias point and the alternating input voltage are set so that there is an output signal for somewhat more than half but less than the entire input voltage cycle. Class B or AB amplifiers for audio applications must be operated in a push-pull configuration to prevent excessive distortion.

An amplifier can also be biased so that there is output current for less than (even much less than) one-half of the input signal voltage cycle. Under these conditions the amplifier is said to be operating in Class C. Because of the significant amplitude clipping (harmonic distortion) produced by the Class C mode, it is not used in audio applications. However, there are radio frequency amplifiers for which this mode is ideally suited.

SPECIAL POWER AMPLIFIER TYPES

The classic amplifier using an active device as we have been discussing has dominated electronics for close to 50 years. Recently developed techniques in semiconductor manufacturing and digital electronics have produced some changes in the basic amplifier types used in audio equipment. We will now look briefly at one of these new types.

MOS VFET Amplifiers

It is generally conceded among audio listeners that the presence of high-order harmonics and modulation products is more disturbing to the listener than low-order harmonics which may add up to the same single harmonic percentage figure. Distortion is covered in Chapter 3 in some detail. The manner in which bipolar transistors operate with fast transient waves leads to the generation of high-order harmonic distortion, even at input levels below the point of clipping a sine wave test signal. This distortion, caused by large amounts of time-delayed negative feedback and carrier storage effects of the bipolar junction transistor, is responsible for audible differences between vacuum tube amplifiers and BJT amplifiers whose power output and overall distortion specifications are identical.

A relatively new solid-state device, the metal-oxide semiconductor *vertical* field-effect transistor (MOS VFET), now makes it possible to design a breed of amplifiers that have the advantages of both BJT and vacuum tube equipment. *Figure 2-13* shows the basic structure of this device. Advantages claimed for the VFET include extremely fast rise and fall times (fast pulse response), availability in N- and P-channel configurations for true complementary circuit designs, high input and low output impedance characteristics, and voltage-controlled rather than current-controlled transfer response.

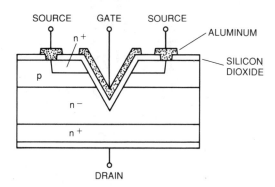

Figure 2-13. Operating structure of a MOS VFET.

POWER SUPPLY

The power supplies for modern audio systems differ greatly depending on such things as the number, quality and power requirements of the circuits that make up the system. Most types of electronic equipment get their power from the 120 VAC, 60 Hz power line. All power supplies have filters that pass the dc (zero Hz) and block the ac ripple. How well the filter smooths the ripple is described by a figure of merit called the *ripple factor*. It is the RMS value of the ripple voltage divided by the average (dc) voltage. When multiplied by 100, the percentage of ripple is given and the ideal value is 0%. Excessive ripple is a result of inadequate or defective filtering and manifests itself as hum in the loudspeakers.

Ideally, the output voltage of a power supply should be a constant value. Unfortunately, this is impossible to achieve because of two factors. First, the line voltage may vary as much as 20%. Second, a change in the current demanded by the power supply load; that is, the circuits that it supplies, causes the output voltage to change. A power supply's ability to regulate its output voltage under changing input voltage and changing load current demand is a measure of its *percent regulation*. To compare the regulation properties of power supplies, the difference in the no-load voltage and the full-load voltage is divided by the full load voltage, then this factor is multiplied by 100 to express it as a percent. An ideal power supply, which cannot be attained in practical circuits, would have zero percent regulation.

The output voltage of the power supply may be regulated by Zener diodes or by a transistorized voltage regulating circuit. A modern audio system may employ an efficient switching-type regulated power supply.

Overloading and Protection

Most power supplies have some means of protection against overloads. It is usually a fuse or circuit breaker which is accessible from the back of the amplifier chassis so it can be easily changed (fuse) or reset (circuit breaker) by the user. Several smaller fuses or "fusible resistor links" may be located inside the power supply to protect other individual circuits from overload damage. These are not intended to be replaced by the user. Expensive audio equipment may have power supply electronic "shutdown" circuits to protect against excessive load current or voltage.

3

KINDS OF DISTORTION

Distortion is an undesired change in the waveform of the original signal as it passes through an audio or video system. The result is unfaithful reproduction of the original signal. This means that the output signal is no longer just an amplified version of the input signal, but has been changed in some way.

TYPES OF DISTORTION

The five types of distortion generally present in amplifiers are: (1) frequency distortion, (2) phase distortion, (3) harmonic distortion, (4) intermodulation distortion, and (5) transient intermodulation distortion.

Frequency distortion occurs when certain frequencies are amplified more or less than others. It is caused by capacitive and inductive effects within a circuit. The frequency response is the audio specification that reveals the degree of frequency distortion present in a circuit or system.

Phase distortion occurs when one frequency component of a complex input signal takes longer to pass through an amplifier or system than another frequency. Though their amplitudes may be equally amplified over the frequency band (that is, no frequency distortion), there may be differential phase shift for the individual frequency components; therefore, the composite signal is changed.

Total harmonic distortion (THD) is probably the most common distortion. The percentage of THD depends upon the magnitude of the generated harmonics. The technique of Fourier analysis may be used to account for and measure the harmonic distortion.

Intermodulation (IM) distortion occurs when combinations of new frequencies are generated by modulation within the amplifier or system. These new frequencies are equal to the sums and differences of integral multiples of the component frequencies of a complex wave.

Transient intermodulation (TIM) distortion occurs principally during loud, high-frequency music passages in solid-state amplifiers that use large amounts of negative feedback to improve frequency response and reduce harmonic distortion.

HARMONIC DISTORTION

A sine wave signal, shown in *Figure 3-1a*, is absolutely pure with only one fundamental frequency component; therefore, it has no harmonic content. A harmonic is an integer (whole number) multiple of the fundamental frequency. For example, a sine wave with a fundamental frequency of 500 Hz would have a second harmonic of 1000 Hz, a third harmonic of 1500 Hz, and so forth. Anything that happens to a sine wave signal of fundamental frequency that acts to change its waveshape will add other signal components to the fundamental frequency signal.

An audio amplifier should not modify the shape of the waveform that it processes. If it does, the resulting harmonic signals will change the character of the sound produced by the speaker.

Harmonic distortion occurs when the amplifying device is operated in a non-linear portion of its transfer curve. An amplifier should operate as much as possible in the linear portion if unpleasant changes in the signal that it is amplifying are to be avoided.

Figures 3-1b and *3-1c* show common, but complex, repetitive waveforms and their frequency content. The square wave shown in *Figure 3-1b* has only odd harmonics beside the fundamental frequency while the sawtooth waveform of *Figure 3-1c* has both even and odd harmonics. Note the reduced amplitudes of the harmonics compared to the fundamental frequency.

Any complex or distorted wave can be better understood when considered as being made up of a combination of signals. Using a method known as *Fourier analysis*, any periodic wave can be represented by three parts: (1) the fundamental frequency, (2) a dc component, and (3) various amplitudes of even and odd order harmonics of the fundamental.

Often the distortion is characterized by a predominance of either even or odd harmonics. If even harmonics are a problem, they can be virtually eliminated by using a push-pull output power amplifier.

The percentage of harmonic distortion depends on the magnitude of the generated harmonics. Of course, 0% distortion is the ideal condition. To verify performance of an amplifier, it is necessary to check distortion at a variety of power levels and at a sufficient number of audio frequencies to make certain that the total harmonic distortion is less than or equal to the distortion specification.

Harmonic distortion can be measured by using various types of test equipment. The most common measurement is total harmonic distortion which is expressed mathematically in the following equation:

$$THD = \frac{(\text{Total Signal} - \text{Fundamental Signal})}{\text{Total Signal}}$$

TRANSFER CURVES AND DISTORTION

A device or system that involves an input and an output signal has transfer characteristics. A plot of the input and output instantaneous signals produces a graph called the transfer curve or transfer function.

Recall that we discussed transfer curves earlier. *Figure 3-2a* shows a linear transfer curve and *Figure 3-2b* shows a non-linear transfer curve. The input signal is plotted on the X or horizontal axis. The resultant output signal is plotted on the Y or vertical axis. The input signal V_{in} is shown varying along a time axis around the input operating point V_{io}. The output signal V_{out} appears at the output varying with time around the output operating point V_{oo}. Two curves are shown in *Figure 3-2a*. Curve #1 represents an amplifier with a gain more than 1. Curve #2 represents an amplifier with a gain less than 1.

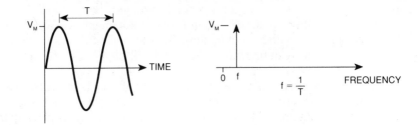

a. A Sinusoidal Signal and Its Amplitude Spectrum

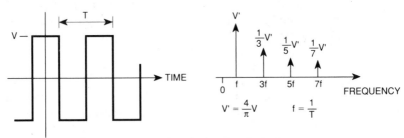

b. A Square Waveform and Its Amplitude Spectrum

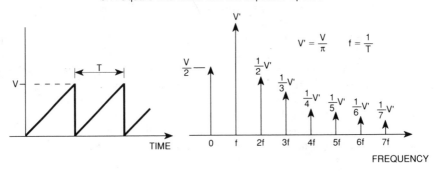

c. A Sawtooth Waveform and Its Amplitude Spectrum

Figure 3-1. Common waveforms and their frequency spectrums.

When input signal V_{in} is applied to the amplifier whose curve is shown in *Figure 3-2a*, an exact reproduction of the input signal is produced at the output without distortion because the transfer curves are linear over the complete range. However, when input signal V_{in} is applied to the amplifier whose curve is shown in *Figure 3-2b*, the output waveform is distorted significantly because the transfer curve is non-linear.

Harmonic Distortion

Distortion of a single frequency input signal produced by a non-linear transfer curve like the curve shown in *Figure 3-2b* is called harmonic distortion. The output signal contains harmonic components of the fundamental signal that were not present in the original input signal. The distorted signal is shown as AV_{out}.

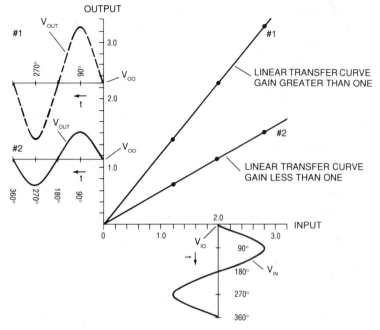

a. Linear Transfer Curve

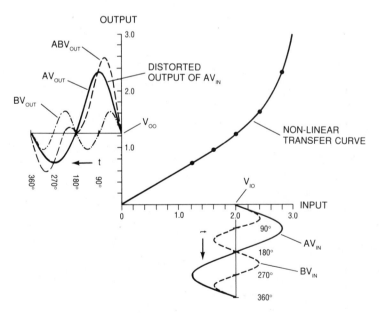

b. Non-Linear Transfer Curve

Figure 3-2. Transfer curves and distortion.

Intermodulation Distortion

When two input signals of different frequencies (AV_{in} and BV_{in}) are passed through the amplifier whose curve is shown in *Figure 3-2b*, then an additional distortion called intermodulation distortion is introduced. This occurs because now the output, ABV_{out}, contains not only harmonics of the fundamental frequency, but also sum or difference frequency components between the two input frequencies. The output waveform cannot be reconstructed without components of the sum and difference frequencies between AV_{in} and BV_{in}. Intermodulation is the production of new frequencies corresponding to the sums and differences of the frequencies of the initial signals.

The percentage of intermodulation distortion can be predicted from harmonic distortion in the system. A system can be relatively free of intermodulation distortion, but generate moderate amounts of harmonic distortion at specific frequencies. The reverse is also true.

Amplitude Distortion

Figure 3-3 demonstrates amplitude or non-linear distortion due to increasing input signal amplitude such that the amplifier output is beyond the linear dynamic range. Amplification of AVin to produce AVout is distortion-free because the amplifier is operating within its linear dynamic range. Increasing the input signal amplitude to BV_{in} (while keeping the frequency the same) causes the amplifier to exceed its linear dynamic range and produces amplitude distortion in the output waveform BV_{out}.

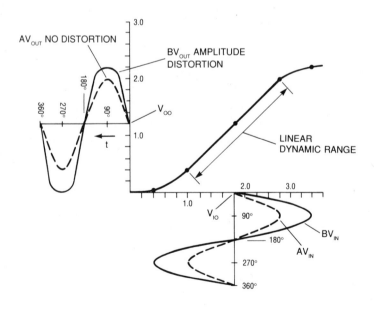

Figure 3-3. Amplitude distortion.

HOW DOES DISTORTION AFFECT THE SOUND OF AN AUDIO SIGNAL?

Music theory addresses this question in detail; however, we will describe here how THD and IM affect what we hear.

THD

When we discussed square waves, we mentioned that when additional frequencies are added to a fundamental frequency, it changes its sound or timbre. Since harmonic distortion adds new frequencies, it causes a change in timbre. When viewed on an instrument that separates frequency components—a spectrum analyzer—these new frequencies cluster around the original frequencies. Some frequencies affect our hearing more than others. The sensitivity of the human ear is highest in the middle and upper regions of the audible spectrum. The harmonic frequencies in this range are distinctly noticeable although their relative amplitudes may be small. The result in the sound is a blur in the original signal.

IM

It is most important to be concerned with IM distortion in equipment intended for use with audible reproduction of complex signals. Intermodulation distortion on audio equipment specifications is usually measured by one of two methods. The most popular method of measurement at the present time is the Society of Motion Picture and Television Engineers (SMPTE) modulation method. The specific tones and level ratios are those recommended by the Institute of High Fidelity Manufacturers (IHFM).

The first method uses a low frequency (60 Hz) with a much higher frequency (either 6 kHz or 7 kHz), and detects the kind of IM that occurs when high-level low frequencies are present. It was a kind of distortion prevalent in early "talking pictures."

The second method, originated in Europe by the CCITT (Comite Consultatif International Telephonique Et Telegraphique), uses two high frequencies (6 kHz and 7 kHz) which generates a 1 kHz difference frequency, not present in the input. This method measures the kind of distortion caused by interaction (intermodulation) between higher frequencies.

The two methods detect IM distortion over different portions of the frequency spectrum. The first over the lower frequency portion and the second over the higher frequency portion.

In chapter 1, we discussed how the tone quality or timbre of a sound is effected by the harmonically related frequencies contained in the sound. The major difference between harmonic distortion and intermodulation distortion is that IM results in new *harmonically unrelated* frequencies generated.

TRANSIENT INTERMODULATION DISTORTION

Audio engineers thought that they had mastered all of the distortions and that audio hi-fi equipment had reached the highest possible level. They were about to settle back with the knowledge that they had succeeded in reducing harmonic distortion and intermodulation distortion to almost unmeasurable, and certainly inaudible, levels. However, this satisfaction was rudely interrupted by a newcomer—the transistor amplifier—which was introduced into the music world of the late 1950s and early 1960s. It had a different sound, and the critical ear of the professional musician chose the sound of the vacuum tube amplifier every time over a transistor amplifier.

Audio specialists began investigating this phenomenon. Results of the accepted steady-state IM and THD tests proved that a transistor amplifier had as good or better specifications than a vacuum tube amplifier of similar design. However, the investigators found that another type of distortion, which was peculiar to the transistor, was causing the difference in sound. Remember that we discussed that music has a transient nature; that is, its waveform is characterized by a short term impulse with a steep wavefront and a very fast decay. The transistors being used at that time were not reproducing these transients correctly, and the resultant sound had less than hi-fi quality. This particular sound was appropriately called "transistor sound," and this type of distortion was called *transient intermodulation distortion* .

Much attention has been given to this form of audio distortion in recent years. Unlike THD and IM, it does not lend itself to simple measurement and a universal industry measurement standard has not, as yet, been established.

FREQUENCY AND PHASE DISTORTION

Amplitude Frequency Response

Frequency distortion results when the amplitude of the output of a system or a device varies as the frequency of the input varies while the amplitude of the input is held constant. Thus, for an amplifier, frequency distortion occurs when certain frequencies are amplified more or less than others.

As we saw in Chapter 1, music and speech have many different frequency components. They correspond to the fundamental and the harmonic frequencies produced by the sound source. Usually, the different input signal frequencies have different amplitudes as they enter the system, and the system should maintain the same *relative* amplitudes of these signals as they are processed through the system. Otherwise, the original character (timbre) of the sound will change. The specification that reveals the degree of frequency distortion in a system is its *amplitude frequency response*

Phase Response

The term *phase* is defined as the time relationship between two corresponding points on a repetitive wave. If the period of the wave is expressed in angular units (for example, 360 degrees), then the phase may be expressed as a phase angle. Phase distortion occurs when one frequency component of a complex input signal takes a longer time to pass through a system than another frequency component. Though their relative amplitudes are not changed (that is, no frequency distortion), a differential phase shift for the individual frequency components occurs and the shape of the composite signal is changed.

Bode Plot

The composite frequency response is the combination of the amplitude response and the phase response. These response functions can be calculated with circuit analysis or measured with instruments. A graphical technique, named after H.W. Bode of Bell Laboratories who introduced the concept, plays a major role in circuit

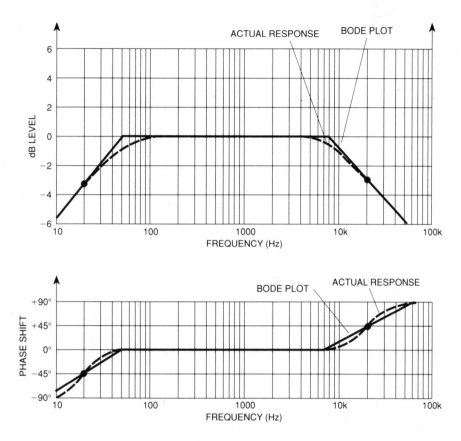

Figure 3-4. A Bode plot.

analysis. This technique, which is a good straight-line approximation of the amplitude response and the phase response plotted on a logarithmic scale of frequency, is shown in *Figure 3-4*. By knowing the slope of the amplitude response and the phase response, the straight lines can be plotted through the corner frequencies at the low end and high end of the frequency spectrum. The −3 dB amplitude response corresponds to the 45 degree angle (lead and lag) points on the phase response plot. The slope of the amplitude response is typically expressed in dB per octave or dB per decade.

The amplitude response is the specification given most frequently for a system. It is commonly referred to simply as the frequency response. *Figure 3-5* shows a typical plot of an audio amplifier's frequency response with a constant amplitude input signal. *Figure 3-4* is for simple 6 dB per octave roll-offs at each end. Bode plots get more complex when the roll-off is greater.

At low frequencies, the output voltage decreases because of series coupling capacitance. At high frequencies, the output voltage decreases because of the parallel (shunt) capacitance of stray wiring and the limitations of transistor and integrated circuits. In the middle range of frequencies, the amplifier produces its maximum output and the frequency response is "flat."

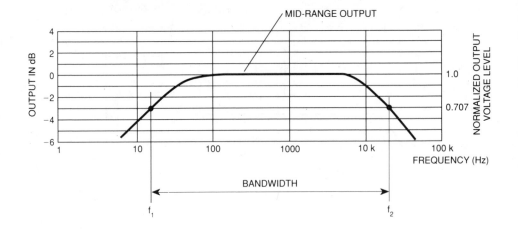

Figure 3-5. An amplifier frequency response curve.

The critical frequencies of an amplifier are the frequencies where the output voltage drops to 0.707 of the middle range output. A decrease of the voltage by a factor of 0.707 is equivalent to -3 dB, so these critical frequencies are often referred to as the *3 dB down points* Other names for these critical frequencies are the *cutoff* or *rolloff* frequencies. An amplifier usually has two of these critical frequencies, shown as f_1 and f_2 in *Figure 3-5.* The range of frequencies between f_1 and f_2 is called the passband, or bandwidth.

Standards and Recommendations

The frequency response of an amplifier can be measured with the test setup depicted in *Figure 3-6.* An ideal amplifier is one in which all frequencies pass through with equal amplification; that is, it has a flat response. The *EIA Standard Methods of Measurement for Audio Amplifiers* states that the rated frequency response is "the frequency range over which the amplitude response does not vary more than ±3 dB from the amplitude at 1000 Hz." Also, the EIA Standard recommends that "the frequency response be measured at a power output *not higher than* 10 dB below the rated power output of the amplifier and *not lower than* 20 dB above residual hum and noise." Some other authorities define stereo audio amplifiers as having a frequency response from 20 Hz to 20 kHz within ±1 dB and less than 1% THD at maximum rated power output.

The output measurements must be taken at whatever power level condition the manufacturer intended in the published specifications, while maintaining a constant signal input voltage level at all frequencies. The resultant output voltages can be used as the data to plot a frequency response curve calibrated in either absolute voltage terms or in relative decibels referenced to the value at 1000 Hz. The largest frequency increment for each measurement point for the plot should not be greater than one octave (that is, the next higher frequency is two times the current frequency). However, the smaller the frequency increment, the more accurate the plot will be.

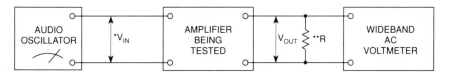

*V_{IN} CONSTANT FOR ALL FREQUENCIES
**R ADJUSTED TO APPROPRIATE POWER LEVEL

Figure 3-6. Test setup to measure frequency response.

Tone Control

The tone control provides a way for the listener to alter the frequency response of the amplifier so the sound is pleasing to the listener. Most tone controls are designed so the listener can make separate level adjustments in the bass, mid-range, and treble sounds. Adjustment of the tone controls can correct for speaker response limits and room resonance problems, or simply tailor the sound to suit the listener's taste.

Figure 3-7 shows the typical effect that tone controls have on an amplifier. The tone control causes a 12 dB insertion loss in the amplifier path so more overall amplifier gain is required to recover this loss. The bass adjustment can then decrease this loss to 0 dB at 20 cycles (providing significant increase in bass response) or increase the loss to 24 dB (providing hardly any base response at all). Similar response changes can be made at the high frequency end with the treble control increasing response from −12 dB to 0 dB at 20 KHz or decreasing response to −24 dB.

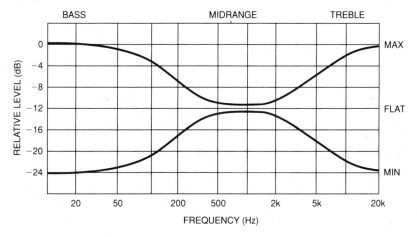

Figure 3-7. Tone control circuit response.

Three popular tone control circuits are shown in *Figure 3-8*. The circuit in *Figure 3-8a* simply reduces treble frequencies which gives the listener the perception of increased bass. The circuits of *Figure 3-8b* and *3-8c* produce response results as indicated in *Figure 3-7*. The circuit in *Figure 3-8b* is usually in the signal path between amplifier stages, while that in *Figure 3-8c* is in a path that includes feedback. The circuits must be inserted at a point in the amplifier system that is of sufficient signal level so that the amplifier stages remain in their linear range.

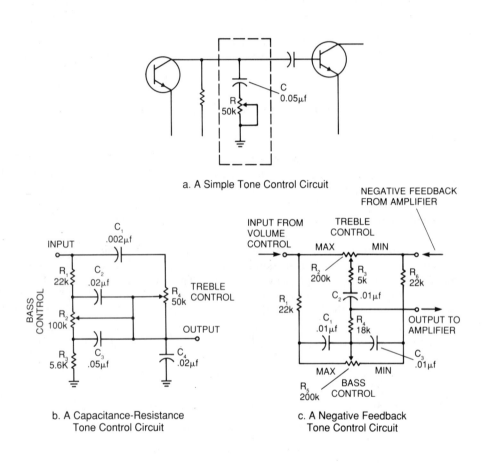

a. A Simple Tone Control Circuit

b. A Capacitance-Resistance Tone Control Circuit

c. A Negative Feedback Tone Control Circuit

Figure 3-8. Tone control circuits.

SUMMARY

In this chapter, we have discussed the kinds of distortion and what causes a particular distortion in an amplifier. In the next chapter, we will discuss transducers—the sensors that convert sound to electrical energy or convert electrical, magnetic or optical energy to sound.

4

SOUND TRANSDUCERS

An important topic in *Making Sense of Sound* is the concept of the *transducer*. A transducer is any device that is capable of changing one form of energy into another form of energy.

A musical instrument, like the guitar in *Figure 4-1*, is a transducer. When the strings are plucked, they vibrate and create pressure waves of sound in the air that are increased in intensity by the resonance of the hollow body of wood. The microphone is another transducer shown in *Figure 4-1*. It converts sound waves into a series of corresponding electrical voltages. These voltages can then be electronically processed; that is, amplified, recorded, and modified. They can be converted back into sound waves by another transducer—the speaker.

In order to record, reproduce or transmit voice or music sounds by radio or television, it is necessary that the audible sounds be converted to electrical signals. The conversion of sound waves to electrical signals or vice versa requires the use of a device known as an *electro-acoustic transducer*. In this chapter we will consider several common types of these transducers. We will begin with the microphone.

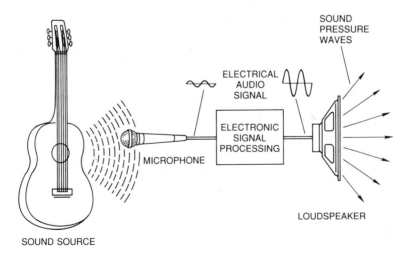

Figure 4-1. The sound chain showing electro-acoustic transducers: a guitar producing sound, a microphone, electronic signal processing, and a loudspeaker.

MICROPHONES

The microphone is a type of electro-acoustic transducer used to convert sound waves to electrical signals. Actually, it changes acoustical energy to mechanical energy and then to electrical energy. There are many different types of microphones, but practically all of them have certain characteristics in common. Although a microphone may seem simple to its user, its performance greatly depends upon proper selection, connection and use.

Principles of Microphones

The four basic parts of any microphone are the transducer element, the outer housing, the cable and the connector, as illustrated in *Figure 4-2*. The transducer element is the most important component because that is where the electrical signal is generated. The transducer may be further divided into the diaphragm and the conversion element. The type of transducer element in the microphone determines its type and basic characteristics. The sound waves are converted into mechanical motion by the diaphragm. This motion is then converted into an electrical signal by the conversion element.

Types of Microphones

Of the several common varieties that exist, the transducer elements can be classified according to their basic principle of operation. The first type, piezoelectric, is shown in *Figure 4-2*.

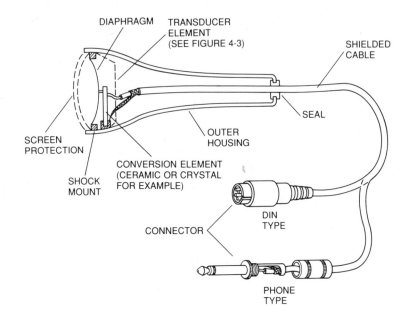

Figure 4-2. The parts of a microphone.

Piezoelectric

The piezoelectric (which means "pressure electricity") effect is a property of certain crystals and ceramics. When the crystal or ceramic element is bent, an electrical voltage is generated in proportion to the amount of bend. The sound moves the diaphragm, which moves the crystal. Because it is low in cost and reasonably good in quality, it is a popular choice in inexpensive equipment.

Variable Resistance

Perhaps the most common microphone is the single-button carbon microphone, which is shown in *Figure 4-3a*. It has a variable resistance transducer element which has been used for years in the telephone. Sound waves vibrate the diaphragm which compresses or decompresses the carbon granules, thereby varying their resistance. The varying resistance causes varying current in the electrical circuit so the sound is converted into electrical signals. Although the carbon microphone does not have the most desirable reproduction characteristics, it is inexpensive, rugged and highly reliable.

Moving-Coil Induction

The microphone that operates on the moving-coil induction principle is shown in *Figure 4-3b*. Its uses a transducer element that is commonly called a dynamic element. It has a small coil of fine wire wound on a form which is attached to the diaphragm. The coil is positioned in the field of a strong permanent magnet. When a sound wave moves the diaphragm and coil, a current is induced in the coil proportional to the sound wave.

Capacitor

The transducer element of the capacitor microphone (*Figure 4-3c*) is made of a metal diaphragm suspended from, and insulated from, a fixed metal backplate. A fixed dc voltage is applied through a load resistor between the diaphragm and the backplate. When the diaphragm is moved by a sound wave, the capacitance varies

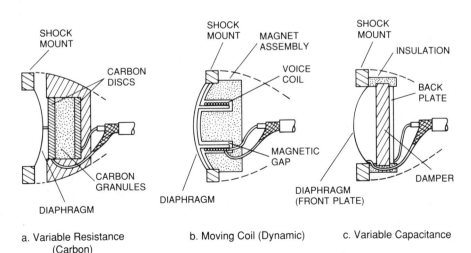

a. Variable Resistance (Carbon) b. Moving Coil (Dynamic) c. Variable Capacitance

Figure 4-3. Basic types of microphones.

43

which causes the voltage across it to vary directly with the sound wave. The "electret" microphone is a special type of capacitor microphone that has its own charge source built in, thereby eliminating the need for an external voltage source. The capacitor microphone, originally called the condenser microphone, generally provides a smooth detailed sound with a very wide frequency response.

Microphone Characteristics and Ratings

The performance of a microphone is measured mainly by its sensitivity, frequency response and directional pickup pattern. Other performance characteristics to be considered are impedance, noise and distortion.

Sensitivity

Sensitivity is a measure of the amount of output signal voltage produced when a standard reference level (74 dB SPL) of sound pressure signal at 1000 Hz is applied to the microphone. A very sensitive microphone produces a relatively high output voltage for a given sound source loudness. Microphones with a low sensitivity may require a preamplifier to increase the signal strength above the noise level.

Frequency Response

Frequency response is the range of frequencies that the microphone can process or reproduce without a change in level, within a tolerance range such as ±3 dB. A frequency response curve is a graph of the output level plotted in dB on the vertical scale against frequency on the horizontal scale, as shown in *Figure 4-4*. If an accurate or natural sound is desired when it is reproduced, the frequency response of the microphone should extend at least over the frequency range of the sound signal that it is to pick up. A microphone with a "flat" extended response reproduces the fundamental frequencies and the harmonics in the same proportion as the sound source. The microphone whose response is shown in *Figure 4-4* has a "presence peak" around 5 kHz. This causes it to emphasize the higher harmonics which gives it a crisp, articulate sound.

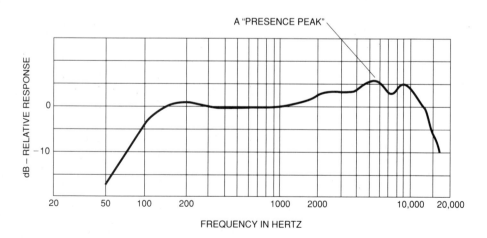

Figure 4-4. A microphone frequency response curve.

Pickup Pattern

Microphones also exhibit a *directional response* in their pickup characteristics. This directional pickup response pattern partly determines its performance and use. The simplest pattern is omni-directional, as shown in the polar plot of *Figure 4-5*. A omni-directional microphone has about equal sensitivity for sound waves in all directions. The other plot shown in *Figure 4-5* is a cardioid pattern, so called because it resembles the shape of a heart. Cardioid pickup pattern microphones are very popular because they allow the performer to be farther away from the microphone without having serious interference problems from sounds on the opposite side of the microphone.

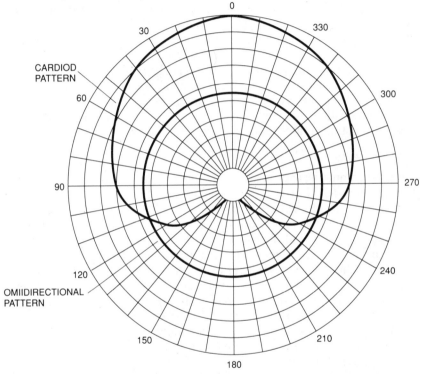

Figure 4-5. Microphone directional pickup response patterns.

Impedance

The impedance of a microphone is classified as low if it's 600 ohms or less. Low-impedance microphones should use a balanced line shielded cable. High-impedance microphones are typically above 5,000 ohms, and use a shielded, unbalanced line cable. Low-impedance microphones are preferred for long cable runs to minimize noise and hum pickup, and high-frequency loss.

Noise

The *equivalent noise level* is the electrical noise that a microphone produces with no acoustic input. It is equivalent to the output that an equivalent sound source would produce. We describe what this means later.

Distortion

The most significant distortion specification of a microphone is the *maximum sound pressure level*. Refer to *Figure 1-6* and notice that normal conversation at one foot measures about 70 dB SPL. Maximum SPL is the sound level at which the microphone's output produces a total harmonic distortion (THD) of 3% (see Chapter 3). A high-quality dynamic microphone can handle a sound pressure level of 150 dB SPL or more.

SPEAKERS

Most modern-day speakers have evolved from a cross between the headset used with the early crystal radio receivers and the small vibrating diaphragm connected to the stylus and the wooden horn on Thomas Edison's phonograph. As electronic audio equipment improved, speakers became more powerful and efficient as well as higher in quality and complexity. The final sound of all stereo and other audio equipment depends upon the performance of the speaker system. The term *speaker* can refer to a single speaker or an enclosure containing several speakers interconnected through an electronic crossover network. The heart of a speaker is its driver. It is the electro-acoustical transducer that converts the electrical input signals to mechanical motion that creates the sound pressure waves.

Dynamic Drivers

The driver most commonly used in audio equipment is the dynamic (moving-coil) type shown in *Figure 4-6*. The reason for the popularity of the electrodynamic driver is that it can be manufactured at a fairly low cost and still produce reasonably good quality sound when installed in a proper enclosure. A fixed magnetic field is produced by a powdered metal alloy or ceramic permanent magnet. The electrical signals from the amplifier produce an alternating magnetic field in the voice coil. The interaction of the two magnetic fields causes the voice coil to move. Since the speaker cone is physically attached to the voice coil, the cone also moves and thus moves the air around it to create sound waves. The voice coil and the small end of the cone are supported by the flexible spider. The large end of the cone is supported by the flexible suspension system called the surround.

The size of the driver is related to the range of audio frequencies for which it is used. Large drivers from 10 to 20 inches in diameter are called *woofers* and are used for the lower frequencies from about 20 Hz to 2000 Hz. The *mid-range* drivers are about 3 to 8 inches in diameter and are used for the middle frequencies from about 800 Hz to 10 kHz. An inexpensive sound system may have only a mid-range driver. The high frequency drivers, called *tweeters*, have cone diameters as small as 1 inch and produce the frequencies from about 4 kHz to 20 kHz. With a properly designed system using all three driver types, the complete audio frequency spectrum can be reproduced.

Piezoelectric and Electrostatic Drivers

A piezoelectric driver is opposite to the piezoelectric microphone discussed previously. When an electrical signal is applied to the crystal, the crystal bends and moves the diaphragm coupled to it and produces sound. Such a driver can faithfully follow high frequencies up to 30 kHz; thus, it is an efficient tweeter.

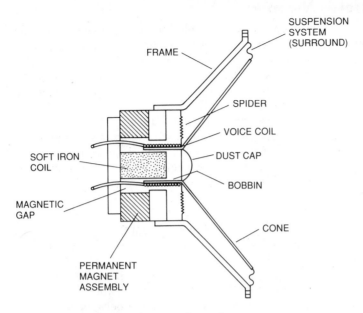

Figure 4-6. Dynamic speaker.

The electrostatic speaker also is constructed much like its microphone counterpart, but used in reverse. The back plate is made of rigid aluminum, usually semicircular in shape. The diaphragm is the front plate and consists of a metallic film deposited on an insulating film acting as the dielectric. The plates are charged (or biased) with a high polarizing dc voltage which sets up a stress between the plates. The audio voltage from the amplifier is then superimposed on the dc voltage to produce a changing electrostatic field which causes the diaphragm to move back and forth.

In a newer adaptation of this original electrostatic design, the front and back charged plates are rigid and contain many small holes. Between these plates, and insulated from them, is a thin conductive diaphragm powered by the audio signal. This gives a push-pull effect which improves linearity, and therefore, sound quality. Most electrostatic drivers are large in size and quite expensive. Smaller versions, designed for tweeters only, are used in some better-quality systems to produce sounds into the ultrasonic range. Such sounds are preferred by some listeners.

Enclosures

The enclosure is not only a box that holds the drivers, but it also performs several important purposes in the sound production. It usually improves quality and efficiency. This is accomplished by improving the natural resonance and reducing sound cancellation by actually using the sound from the back of the cone. Some speaker enclosures have airtight seals, and some have openings called ports. For a complete discussion of speakers and enclosures, see *Speakers for Your Home and Automobile* by Gordon McComb, published by Howard W. Sams & Company.

Crossover Networks

Crossover networks are frequency-selective circuits that separate the audio signal into two or three frequency ranges for feeding the various speakers in a speaker system. Most stereo systems use a simple passive crossover as shown in *Figure 4-7a*. This type of crossover has a 6 dB slope. The crossover slope or roll-off is the rate at which the level of the signal changes as a function of frequency measured in dB per octave. We discussed this in Chapter 3.

The coils (inductors) and capacitors function as filters which permit only a limited range of frequencies to pass through. In *Figure 4-7a*, inductor L2 passes low frequencies to the woofer, but blocks the mid-range and high-range frequencies. Capacitor C2 and inductor L1 form a bandpass filter for the mid-range frequencies. Capacitor C1 passes only high frequencies to the tweeter.

Speaker Controls

To balance the sound output of the drivers, a control is sometimes used between the crossover and the mid-range and tweeter drivers. These controls, which are sometimes called "brilliance" controls, are a type of tone control.

In addition, as shown in *Figure 4-7a*, an attenuator pad is used in a speaker system to control output level. It is a resistive network that is used to introduce either a fixed or variable amount of attenuation between a source and a load. A variable attenuator may be as simple as a potentiometer as shown in *Figure 4-7b*(1). It is simple to install and inexpensive, but does not present a constant impedance to the load or the source. The more expensive L-pad and T-pad (*Figures 4-7b*(2) and *4-7b*(3), respectively) provide both variable attenuation and constant impedance. These are used in higher quality speaker systems.

Impedance

Impedance is probably one of the least understood terms used in the audio field. It is often misused in applications of multiple speaker installations. Most present day solid-state power amplifiers are designed to drive loads between 4 and 16 ohms; therefore, one speaker with the correct impedance can be used directly. Exact impedance matching of the speaker system to the solid-state power amplifier is not critical as long as it is in the range of 4 to 16 ohms. The problems arise when multiple speakers are used.

Power imbalance may exist if speakers of different impedances are connected to the same amplifier's output. When speakers (e.g. 8-ohm) are connected in series, the equivalent impedance (16 ohms) is the sum of the individual speaker impedances. If many 8-ohm speakers are connected in series (e.g. three), the total of their impedances (24 ohms) limits the power a power amplifier can deliver.

When two speakers are connected in parallel, and each has the same impedance (e.g. 8 ohms), the equivalent impedance of the group is the impedance of one divided by the number of speakers connected in parallel ($8 \div 2 = 4$ ohms). If many speakers (e.g. four) are connected in parallel, the equivalent impedance ($8 \div 4 = 2$ ohms) may be so low that it overloads the power amplifier. By connecting several speakers in a combination of series and parallel, the equivalent impedance can be kept near 8 ohms, a good typical value.

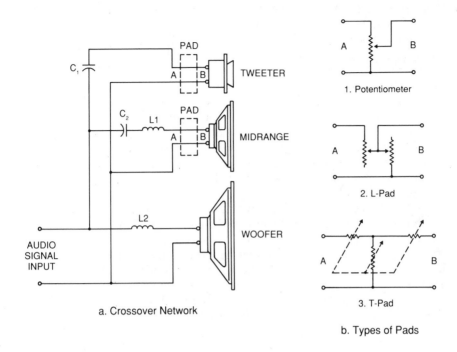

a. Crossover Network

b. Types of Pads

Figure 4-7. A passive crossover network.

Wire Size

Just as the size of a water pipe is an important factor in determining the maximum amount of water that can be delivered, the size of the wires carrying the signal from the power amplifier to the speaker is an important factor in determining the maximum power that can be delivered. Too small a wire increases the effective speaker load impedance as seen by the power amplifier. This affects power loss (efficiency), damping, frequency response and even distortion. The total wire resistance, which depends on the wire size and its length, should be much less than the speaker impedance. A common wire that works well for most stereo systems is American Wire Gauge (AWG) #16 speaker wire or lamp cord. The lamp cord (some-times called "zip" cord) or speaker wire usually has a slight rib on the insulation, or a color code, of one wire to identify the polarity.

Speaker Polarity

Speakers operating with the same system must be driven in phase with each other or the output from one speaker will tend to cancel the output of the other speakers. Speakers are polarized because of the permanent magnet used in conjunction with the voice coil current and its field. A positive polarity signal on one terminal will move the cone outward whereas a negative polarity on the same terminal will move the cone inward. Most speakers are marked with a + or a spot of paint to indicate which terminal will cause the cone to move outward when a positive polarity is applied.

Thus, we see that total system quality sound output depends not only on attention to the driver(s), the enclosure, and the crossover network, but also to the characteristics of the amplifier, the listening area, and interconnection and placement of the speakers.

MAGNETIC TAPE HEADS

One very important transducer for audio systems that we have not mentioned is the magnetic tape head. All magnetic tape recorders/players use at least one head for playing, recording or erasing a signal on a magnetic tape. Many use two heads, and some even use three so that each function has its own head. Whether one, two or three, each head operates the same way. It is simply an electromagnetic transducer that converts an electrical signal to a magnetic field during the recording and erasing process, and converts a magnetic field to an electrical signal during the playback process.

Figure 4-8 shows the essentials of any tape head: the coil and the laminated core with its air gap. The air gap (sometimes called the head gap) is an extremely short distance between the poles of the magnet. It is very important because it concentrates the magnetic field so it can penetrate deeply into the magnetic oxide coating on the tape. This happens because the air gap presents a higher reluctance (resistance) to the magnetic field than the magnetic oxide on the tape, which is bridged across the gap. Therefore, the flux path goes through the tape from one pole piece to the opposite one. There is more about this in Chapter 6.

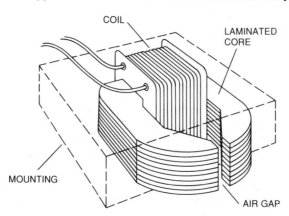

Figure 4-8. A magnetic tape head.

PHONOGRAPH CARTRIDGES

The record player or phonograph, whether a manual turntable or automatic record changer, has been a popular part of sound systems for decades. Its popularity, however, has decreased in recent years because it is being replaced by the cassette tape player and the compact disc player.

The performance of any record player depends on the stylus (needle) movements caused by the rotating record grooves. These movements are converted into an electrical signal by the transducer, which is called a cartridge. It is housed in the tone arm and is either the piezoelectric (ceramic) type or the magnetic (moving-coil) type. They operate using the same principles that we discussed for microphones. The main difference is that a needle replaces the diaphragm to convert mechanical motion to electrical signals through the transducer element. The ceramic element is much less expensive and used in lower cost and lower quality phonographs. The magnetic cartridge is used on almost all high-quality phonographs where full frequency response and low distortion is expected.

OPTICAL TRANSDUCERS

The compact disc (CD) player recovers the audio signal that has been encoded into digital data and stored on the CD. An optical pickup is focused on the disc surface and follows the recorded track to read the stored information. As shown in *Figure 4-9*, the pickup contains a lens system, semiconductor laser source and pickup photodiode. The optical system is a sophisticated mechanism that contains a polarized beam splitter, a diffraction grating, a quarter wavelength plate, and several lenses. The relative intensity of the laser beam reflected back to the photodiode varies according to the presence or absence of pits on the disc. Very high-density storage of digital data (over 2 billion pits along a 3-mile-long track) provides up to 75 minutes of uninterrupted music. The compact disc is also becoming a prominent high-capacity digital storage medium for computers.

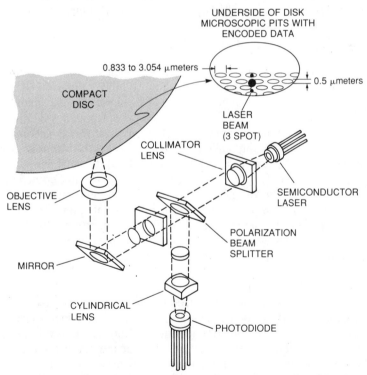

Figure 4-9. An optical transducer pickup used in a compact disc player.

SUMMARY

Now that we understand input and output transducers, we will look at equalizers, mixers, music synthesizers and other new concepts to produce unusual sounds.

5

NEW SOUND CONCEPTS

A decade or so ago, musicians and computer hackers spoke a totally different language. They walked on opposite sides of the street, with the electronic technician/engineer zig-zaging down the middle, independently communicating with both. The computer on a chip changed that. It has brought the two technologies together and has become perhaps the most revolutionary musical tool of the decade. In this chapter, we look at the special effects that can be created—mainly with the microprocessor and high-performance solid-state amplifiers—to produce and enhance the sound of recorded music.

FILTERS

We discussed previously how signals with frequencies across the audio range make up the audio spectrum, and that timbre or tonal quality is determined by the various frequency components contained within a given signal. We can change the timbre or tonal quality of a signal by changing the level of frequency components of the signal in any portion of the spectrum. One way that this is accomplished is by frequency selective circuits called filters. A filter, in its simplest passive form, sharply rejects (attenuates) frequencies outside of its passband. The frequency responses for each of four basic filter circuits are shown in *Figure 5-1*. Therefore, if a filter of the type shown in *Figure 5-1c* is inserted into a signal line, only signals with frequencies between f_1 and f_2 will be present after the filter. All other frequencies will be attenuated to a low level. With operational amplifier integrated circuits, active filters not only attenuate the stop-band of the spectrum, but also amplify and boost the pass-band portion of the spectrum.

EQUALIZERS

Another way of modifying a signal's frequency spectrum is to use an equalizer. As shown in *Figure 5-2a*, an equalizer is essentially a filter, but in most cases it also has an amplifier with a gain adjustment. Equalization affects the tonal quality (frequency components) of a sound by boosting or attenuating selected frequency bands. It is used on telephone lines and in broadcast audio systems to compensate for frequency distortion in the lines, cables or other equipment. It is very important in the professional or home recording studio to help overcome deficiencies in the frequency response of a microphone, musical instrument, or any other equipment in the recording and playback operation. As shown in *Figure 5-2a*, the output of an equalizer can be adjusted to eliminate (cut) frequencies present in the input signal or to boost other frequencies that have been degraded in the input signal.

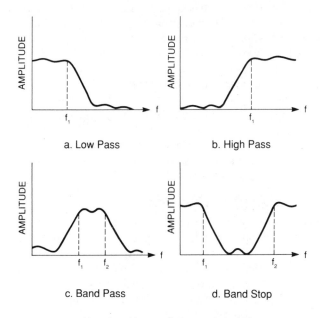

Note: f$_1$ and f$_2$ are called corner frequencies.

Figure 5-1. Frequency response for four basic filter circuits.

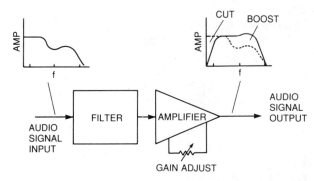

a. Simplified Equalizer

b. Automotive Stereo, Seven-Band,
60-Watt, Equalizer/Booster
(Courtesy of Sherwood)

Figure 5-2. Equalizers.

By connecting several active filters together, with each designed to act on a different (overlapping) portion of the spectrum, we can make a *graphic equalizer*. The effect (cut or boost) that the graphic equalizer has on a particular portion of the spectrum is adjusted by a row of slide potentiometers. These divide the audio spectrum into intervals, usually from five to ten for home equipment and up to 31 for professional studio equipment. The slide potentiometers are arranged side-by-side so their handle positions give an approximation of the actual frequency response curve; thus, the name graphic. Graphic equalizers, usually included in a booster power amplifier like the one shown in *Figure 5-2b*, have become very popular for automobile sound systems.

Equalization can make interesting sound effects and help a voice or single instrument stand out in a recording. It is very useful in eliminating problem frequencies; however, extreme equalization reduces fidelity.

COMPRESSORS AND EXPANDERS

Audio systems commonly have a problem because they do not have enough dynamic range. For example, broadcast AM radio systems typically have a dynamic range of 20-30 dB and FM systems have around 40-50 dB. If program audio with a full dynamic range of 70-90 dB is broadcast, the following can happen: (1) noise from equipment ambient levels and/or the tape itself drowns out the quiet portions in the programming, and/or (2) loud portions will either produce too loud a sound for comfortable listening or be distorted because of overdriving the system. These problems were first controlled by using a compressor.

Compression

Compression keeps the level of the audio signal more constant. It keeps the output signal within the dynamic range of the system though the input signal varies over a large range. It reduces distortion from overload. As shown in *Figure 5-3a*, a compressor acts like an automatic volume control, turning up the system gain when the signal gets too quiet and turning down system gain when the signal gets too loud. The compressor shown in the figure is a variable gain amplifier. When the input signal to the compressor exceeds a predetermined level, called the threshold, the gain is automatically reduced. High-level input signals are amplified with much less gain than low-level signals.

Sometimes a limiter circuit is added to the compressor. When the output level exceeds a threshold level as shown in *Figure 5-3a*, the output stays constant and does not go higher. Or a limiter circuit may be used by itself. The limiter has a faster attack time (1 μs to 1 ms) than the compressor alone (1 ms to 10 ms). For certain programming, the limiter/compressor performs better than the compressor alone.

Expansion

Expansion is the opposite of compression. It increases the dynamic range of the input audio signal. As shown in *Figure 5-3b*, it makes loud signals louder and soft signals softer. The expander, in many applications, performs as a noise reduction processor by diminishing those unwanted signals that are below the selected threshold while passing the desired signals that are above that threshold. A

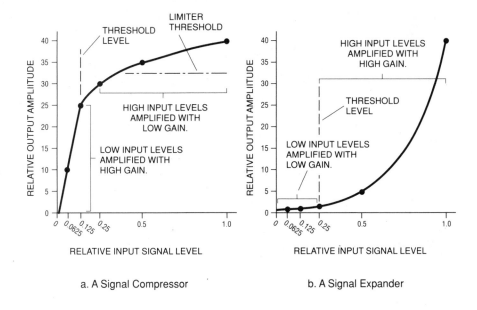

a. A Signal Compressor   b. A Signal Expander

Figure 5-3. Compression and expansion.

combination of compression and expansion processes is called *companding*. Companding is often used in noise reduction systems, which we will discuss further in Chapter 7.

REVERBERATION AND ECHO

Really special effects can be created by using reverberation units and/or an echo chamber. These special effects depend on delaying the signal and combining the delayed and the undelayed signals. *Figure 5-4* shows the difference between reverberation and echo. The delayed signal by itself has no audible effect. However, if we delay the original sound for several milliseconds and combine the delayed sound with the undelayed original, the result is an echo. *Figure 5-4b* shows two echoes arriving from reflections from different sources and at different times.

Reverberation is the persistence of a sound, gradually declining after its origin has stopped. It is deliberately introduced in some audio devices or programs by feedback techniques and a built-in time delay (see *Figure 5-4a*) to impart the feeling of fullness experienced in large auditoriums and concert halls. An echo is a distinct repetition of a sound, whereas reverberation is a continuous decay of a sound.

The spring reverberation unit shown in *Figure 5-5a* has been very popular for three decades in home electronic organs and guitar amplifiers. It uses an electro-mechanical coil-spring device with a transducer on each end to produce the time delay. The output from the first amplifier stage energizes a transducer which drives

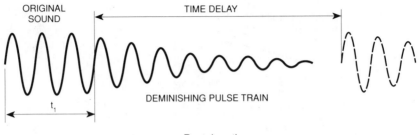

a. Reverberation

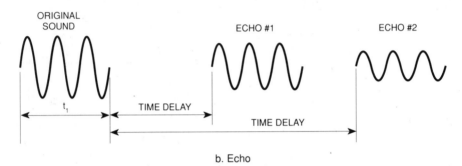

b. Echo

Figure 5-4. Reverberation and echo.

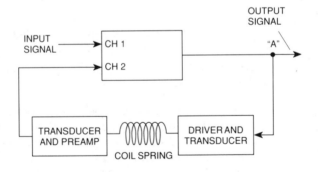

a. Spring Reverberation Unit

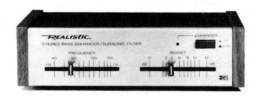

b. Digital Unit
(Courtesy of Radio Shack)

Figure 5-5. Reverberation units.

a wave in the spring corresponding to the original audio signal. At the other end of the spring, the wave that has traveled down the length of the spring energizes another transducer and an amplifier to complete a feedback loop. Notice that the signal is split at point "A," and only a portion is delayed, returned, and combined again, thus producing the reverberation effect. In a professional studio, the spring is usually replaced with a large metal plate, which has a bright sound instead of the somewhat twangy sound produced by the spring.

The low cost and size of a digital reverberation unit like the one in *Figure 5-5b* are making the electromechanical types obsolete. The digital reverberation unit is a microprocessor-based audio effects device that uses a built-in complex algorithm (program) that simulates the acoustics of various concert halls and echo chambers. Such concert-hall sound is referred to as ambience (AMB) in some systems.

MIXERS

A mixer functions as the control center for a recording studio (home or professional) or a live stage performance. It accepts the signals from the microphones, instruments, tape recorders or special effects signal processors. It then combines these signals according to how the operator sets the controls and routes the signals to tape recorders, further signal processors, or the power amplifier. Besides combining the input signals into one or more composite signals, the mixer also amplifies and controls the relative level or volume of each input signal.

Let's follow the signal paths through the two-channel mixer shown in *Figure 5-6*. The input signal goes first to the input attenuator which reduces the level so it will not overdrive the preamp. Sometimes a light-emitting diode (LED) is connected to the output of each preamp to warn against overload. The next stage may be an equalizer to frequency compensate each input signal individually. The fader is next. It is the main level control adjustment to set the relative amplitude of each input. A pan pot adjusts the division of the signal between channels to proportion each input to provide the Channel 1 and Channel 2 stereo image required.

The next function in the mixer signal path is the "aux send" output and the "aux return" input. The signal can be sent to a signal processor for adding echo, reverberation, special effects, and so forth, then the processed signal is returned and blended with the original signal. Next are the mixing amplifier circuits, which are operational amplifiers that sum the signals from the various inputs. These are followed by the master fader, which controls the overall level of all of the output channels.

Level indicators are typically VU meters, though sometimes a column of LEDs or a liquid crystal display column is used. Switches near the meters allow them to be used to monitor signal levels at different points in the mixing process. A five-channel stereo mixer with three "pan" potentiometer microphone controls is shown in *Figure 5-7*. With some practice at the controls—turning knobs, flipping switches, pushing buttons and sliding faders—you are ready to control the production and sound of music.

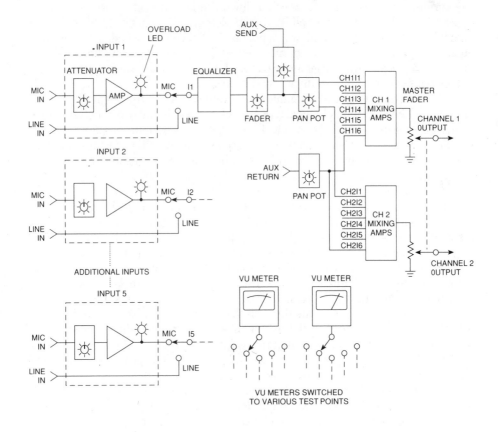

Figure 5-6. Typical circuit of a two-channel mixer.

Figure 5-7. Stereo mixer with five input channels.
(Courtesy of Radio Shack)

CREATING SOUND EFFECTS

You can use commercial sound-effect records and tapes to provide a wide array of different sounds, but by experimenting with your equipment, you can create "new" sounds that may be quite intriguing. Sounds that are usually classified as noise may be utilized to create various special effects. An example is the "fuzz box" popular in rock and roll groups. This is an preamplifier that is designed to badly distort the signal, giving a guitar the characteristic "heavy metal" sound. Try many sources and apply reverberation and echo: you will be surprised at the results.

MUSIC SYNTHESIZERS

In our study of sound thus far, we found in Chapter 1 and in this chapter that the tonal quality of a sound is a result of the sound's component parts—the amplitude, the frequency and the time (phase) relationship. We have called the tonal quality timbre. We found in Chapter 3 that the complex wave of sound could be reduced to its simpler sinusoidal components by Fourier analysis. Any sound wave can be made up of a combination of fundamental and harmonic signals in the proper mixture of amplitude, frequency and phase.

We now introduce two additional ideas: (1) A sound has steady-state parameters for the time interval that it is continuous, and (2) when a sound changes, it has certain transient parameters—parameters that describe the sound while it is changing. Such transient parameters include attack (rise time and rise mode), duration (sustain time), and decay (fall time and fall mode) times.

In music synthesizers, all of these ideas are combined. To synthesize is to assemble or combine separate or subordinate parts into a new form. That's exactly what a music synthesizer does. It does the reverse of Fourier analysis (called Fourier synthesis) and builds a complex sound signal from its basic component parts—in this case, sine and cosine waves. (A cosine wave is displaced 90 degrees in phase from a sine wave). Here's the basic idea: Signal generators (oscillators) produce fundamental frequencies and harmonics which are mixed (using amplifiers and filters) with their amplitudes and phases adjusted according to the coefficients and phases dictated by the Fourier analysis. The resultant envelope of sound sounds like (synthesizes) the musical instrument sound desired.

Basic Operation

Figure 5-8 describes a music synthesizer in block diagram form. There are three basic modules—a generator, a modifier, and a controller. Each separately alters the sound envelope either in frequency, amplitude, phase, or transient parameters to contribute to the musical tone desired. All modules are digitally controlled by a microprocessor system inside the synthesizer. The generator is usually a Digitally Controlled Oscillator (DCO) that directly generates the original signal that is used as the fundamental for the sounds created by the synthesizer. The keyboard tells the DCOs what pitch to produce. The audio signal is altered by modifiers which may include a Digitally Controlled Waveshaper (DCW), a Digitally Controlled Amplifier (DCA), differentiators and integrators, and various modulators and rectifiers.

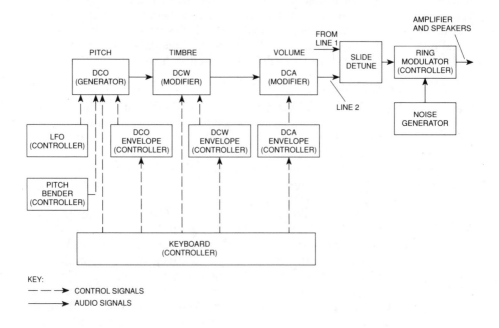

Figure 5-8. Typical music synthesizer block diagram.

The DCW varies the timbre of the sound by modifying the harmonic content of the tone produced by the DCO. The DCA modifies the amplitude of the signal. If the envelope is passed through an integrator module (which is a low-pass filter), the rise and fall times will be increased; therefore, the attack and decay times will be lengthened. A differentiator module (high-pass filter) will accent the higher frequency harmonics and "peaks" the envelope.

Controller module examples are the Low Frequency Oscillator (LFO), Pitch Bender, and Ring Modulator. These are used to modulate (vary one wave with another) the tone generated by the DCO and produce tremolo (amplitude modulation), vibrato (frequency modulation) or portamento (the pitch glides from one note to the next) effects on the synthesizer. Tremolo and vibrato may be combined or used separately, and either or both may be used with portamento. The Ring Modulator is a timbre modifier that greatly increases the number of sounds you can create. When two sound signals are combined in the Ring Modulator, sum and difference frequencies are produced, greatly increasing the number of harmonics contained in the two sounds.

An audio tone can be modified by rectification, which also may be called clipping or limiting. A smooth tone, which is nearly a pure sine wave with no harmonics, becomes raspy sounding when clipped by a rectifier, thereby changing its timbre. Most synthesizers contain a clipper or limiter.

Creating Percussion

A synthesizer contains a random noise generator which is used to produce various drum sounds. A noise signal is comprised of all audio frequencies at constantly varying amplitudes, therefore, it has no definable pitch or timbre. If a second-order (two-pole) filter that has a high Q (low loss) is used after the noise generator, it simulates a drum. This is also called a percussion waveform. If it is repeated at a predetermined rate, it is called a repeat-percussion waveform, which constitutes the basic rhythm section of the synthesizer. A music synthesizer, commonly called a "keyboard," with all of the features we have discussed and more is shown in *Figure 5-9.*

Figure 5-9. Music synthesizer (keyboard) capable of dual-tone mixing of 20 different tones.
(Courtesy of Radio Shack)

Programming the Synthesizer

Synthesizers and computers use the same type of microprocessors. This provides a common meeting ground. Not only can synthesizers be interfaced with computers, but synthesizers also can be interfaced with other compatible synthesizers. The early problem was that each synthesizer manufacturer was using a different microprocessor, which required a different language and protocol set. This problem was overcome when the electronic music industry agreed upon and implemented a standard called the Musical Instrument Digital Interface (MIDI). The potential number of MIDI applications is virtually limitless. For instance, music programs can be uploaded and downloaded to data disks and, by using modems and telephone lines, they can be sent between users. This new "tech-art" has not yet crystallized into an established form—but it may—or it may evolve into something even better than visualized presently.

6

RECORDING
AND
PLAYBACK

The recording and playback industry of today is experiencing an evolutionary process that has undergone a monumental period of change and growth. This process has had an impact on all of the entertainment media. It has resulted from advances in recording technology as well as a maturing in the attitude of both the professionals in the industry and the consuming public. The function of any recording device, audio or video, is to act as a memory or storage facility for information and to reproduce the sound information as closely as possible to the original signal. Recording on magnetic tape is at this time one of the most widely accepted means of accomplishing this process.

TAPE RECORDING

Since the beginning of the electronic audio industry, magnetic tape recording has been the mainstay for the storage of audio signals. A modern magnetic tape system with its ability to write, read and erase audio information has become a standard, and important, high-quality source of music for most stereo music systems.

As we discussed briefly in Chapter 4, during the recording process, a magnetic tape head in a recorder converts audio electrical signals into magnetic fields that are imprinted onto magnetic tape as the tape passes over the head. The highly improved magnetic tape in use today is composed of several layers of material as shown in *Figure 6-1*, each performing a specific function. Most tapes have a mylar® or polyester base with a thin coat of magnetic material, usually gamma ferric oxide or chromium dioxide particles. It is this magnetic layer with its tiny magnetic particles called domains which is responsible for the recording and playback process. *Figure 6-2* shows that these particles have random magnetic orientation in unmagnetized tape, but they are aligned into definite magnetic patterns by the magnetic field produced by the recording head.

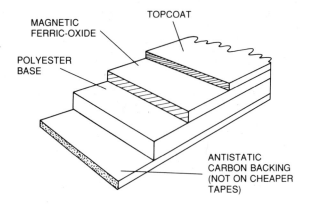

Figure 6-1. The structural layers of magnetic tape.

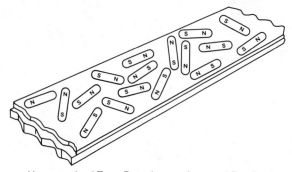

a. Unmagnetized Tape Domains are Arranged Randomly.

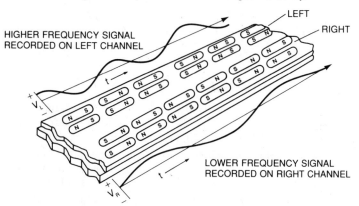

b. Magnetized Tape Domains are Arranged Orderly.

Figure 6-2. The orientation of the magnetic domains of the magnetic oxide.

Tape Coatings

Ferric oxide has been the common coating for years because of its very low price. Chromium dioxide (CrO_2), developed by Dupont about 1970, has a better signal-to-noise (S/N) ratio and a considerably improved high-frequency response, especially at slow tape speed (1-7/8 inches per second). A disadvantage of chromium dioxide is that higher signal levels are needed to record and erase the tape. Newer tape decks, like the one shown in *Figure 6-3*, have a special switch setting for chromium dioxide tape that increases the magnetic field strength and adds special equalization for a flat frequency response during playback. Because of the improved low-speed performance, chromium dioxide is becoming popular in better quality cassette tape systems. However, new double-layered tapes are being developed that combine the best qualities of both ferric oxide (good low-frequency response) and chromium dioxide (good high-frequency response and low noise).

Figure 6-3. A modern stereo dual-cassette tape deck with selection of tape bias (metal, CrO_2, normal).
(Courtesy of Scott)

Standard Track Placement

The tracks on the recording tape are the paths or specific sections used for each channel recorded. Tape recorder heads are available in different track formats. *Figure 6-4* shows the track placement and relative widths for the 1/4-inch tape used for home reel-to-reel and 1/8-inch tape used for cassettes. The 1/4-inch reel-to-reel and the cassette can be turned over after playing one side to make use of the second two tracks. If all other factors are the same, the wider the track, the greater the S/N ratio. Doubling the track width improves the S/N ratio by 3 dB. Professional analog audio tape recorders are available with tape widths up to 2 inches wide and up to 24 tracks (channels). The small unused portion of tape between the tracks improves channel separation; that is, it reduces crosstalk between the channels. It also provides some tolerance for differences in head/track positioning between machines.

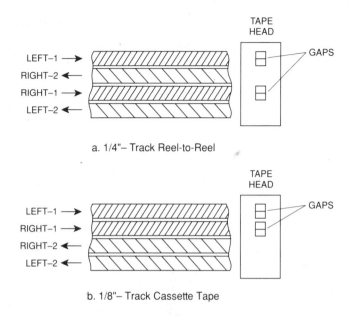

Figure 6-4. Track widths and placements for 1/4-inch and 1/8-inch magnetic tape.

Tape Transports and Drives

The function of the tape transport system is to move the tape past the heads. It is the assembly of the tape recorder on which the motor (or motors), speed control, capstan, tape guides, and tape reel spindles are mounted. During recording and playback, the transport should hold the heads against the tape with a constant tension and move the tape past the heads at a constant speed. During rewind and fast forward, the transport moves the heads away from the tape and winds the tape rapidly from one reel to the other.

Figure 6-5 shows the transport system of a cassette tape recorder. The *capstan* is a small metal shaft driven by the motor at a constant speed. The tape is held firmly against the capstan by the *pinch roller*. As the capstan rotates, it pulls the tape past the heads (erase and record/playback in this machine) at a constant speed. The transport has other rollers to guide the tape and has tension arms to reduce tape speed variations, which cause audible fluctuations called wow and flutter. Wow refers to relatively low cyclic deviations (about 1 hertz), while flutter usually refers to higher deviations (about 10 hertz). Reel-to-reel transports may be more sophisticated with external reels, separate record and playback heads, better tension and motor controls for tape speed and position control.

Control Systems

The newer tape systems use a combination of mechanical and electric/electronic controls to operate the drive system. Automatic switching is used in many systems to provide the play, record, rewind, fast forward and stop functions.

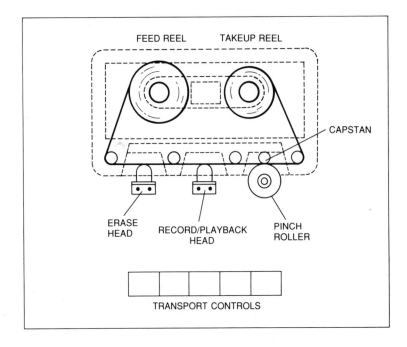

Figure 6-5. A cassette tape transport system.

In many systems, either an automatic shutoff or a tape reversal function controls the transport mechanism when it reaches either end. One of two methods is usually used to sense the tape end. In one method, a metallic strip on the end of the tape completes an electrical circuit across two terminals which are in contact with the tape. The disadvantage of this method is that a tape with the metallic strip must be used. The other method is independent of the tape because the tape transport mechanism senses the increased tension in the tape when it reaches the end. A disadvantage (or perhaps it's an advantage) is that the mechanism can be activated by momentary binding in the tape cassette.

Tape Handling and Storage

Careful handling and storage of tape cassettes and reels is essential to avoid damaging the tape or the signals recorded on it. Improper handling or storage can cause the tape to become dirty, to stretch or shrink, to be accidentally erased, or to *print-through*. Print-through is the transfer of a magnetic signal from one layer of tape to the next, causing an echo. This problem is more common in very thin 0.5-mil or 0.25-mil tapes and in recordings with long, silent passages. The preferred storage conditions are 60° to 75° Fahrenheit at 35% to 50% relative humidity. Many cassette and eight-track tapes have been destroyed by heat in an automobile, especially when left lying on the dash or the rear window ledge.

Magnetic Field Erasure

A common way that tapes are destroyed is accidental erasure by magnetic fields. Permanent magnets on speakers, tools, kitchen decorations or magnetic door-catches have enough magnetic strength to cause partial erasure if they touch or come close to the tape. Electromagnets in telephones and many electric appliances (especially those that contain an electric motor) should be kept away from the tapes. The field of a magnet decreases proportionally to the square of the distance from the magnet, so a distance of a few inches will prevent accidental erasure. Storing tapes in a metal box will protect them from stray magnetic fields.

Troubleshooting Tape Recorder Problems

Magnetic tape heads are made from a magnetically soft metal alloy. This means that the head does not readily retain magnetism but acts as an excellent conductor of flux. It does, however, retain a small amount of residual magnetism, which can erase signals recorded on the tape, especially high frequency signals. A high-frequency hissing noise is an indication that the heads need to be degaussed (demagnetized). It is important that the head be degaussed after 30 to 40 hours of use. Most electronic stores sell demagnetizers (operating instructions are included). Dirty tape heads are one of the most common reasons for a reduction in frequency response and signal level. The heads should be cleaned periodically by placing a few drops of head cleaning fluid or alcohol on a cotton swab and wiping the tape contact areas of all heads. Many tape decks are brought in for service when all they need is a good head cleaning and degaussing.

TURNTABLES AND RECORD CHANGERS

A turntable or a record changer, along with an amplifier and a speaker, make a phonograph or record player system. This particular piece of home audio entertainment equipment has maintained, until recently, a place of high popularity with the listening public. The basic operation of both the turntable and the record changer depends on the stylus of a pickup cartridge to ride in the grove cut into a plastic disc, called a record, while the record rotates. The stylus/pickup cartridge combination converts vibrations imprinted by the recorded signal and picked up from the record grooves into an electrical signal which is amplified and converted into sound.

The turntable has two main systems: (1) the *sensing system* which includes the tone arm, stylus, cartridge and the record disc itself; and (2) the *drive system* which includes the power supply, motor, platter (which supports the record), and a drive link between the motor and platter. *Figure 6-6a* shows a state-of-the-art, high-performance turntable. When the turntable has a mechanism for automatically changing records stacked on the spindle, it is called an automatic record changer.

Drive Systems and Speed Controls

There are three basic types of drive links: idler wheel, belt, and direct drive. The drive system of a turntable should turn the platter without producing either electrical or audible noise. Variations in the platter speed produce wow and flutter, just as in the tape system discussed above, which are usually caused by a worn idler drive wheel or drive belt which loses friction and slips.

Rumble

Rumble is produced by very low-frequency mechanical vibrations in the turntable which may be either internally produced (from the motor, idler wheel, or platter) or from an external source. Good quality turntables have rubber or spring suspension systems that reduce the rumble. Rumble is specified as a S/N ratio in decibels. When rumble is very small, the ratio is a large negative number—the larger the better (at least -50 dB is common).

Speed Control

The motors that have been used for phonographs for years are the induction and the synchronous types. The simple induction motor depends on the line voltage to remain constant in order for its speed to be correct. A decrease in the line voltage results in a decrease in speed. The synchronous motor is an improvement because its speed is synchronized to the 60 Hz line frequency for exact speed operation. Its speed does not depend on the voltage or the load on the motor (within design limits). Higher quality turntables use direct-drive. The dc motor's shaft is directly connected to the platter so there is no slippage, and a feedback loop and servo-control system holds the motor's speed constant. The turntable shown in *Figure 6-6a* has such a drive system.

The record drop, recycle control, tone arm movement, and the shut-off switch of an automatic record changer are all automatically controlled. The changer shown in *Figure 6-6b* has a belt drive and a record drop spindle that holds four records.

Tone Arm

The tone arm holds the cartridge so that the stylus maintains proper tracking pressure and tracking angle on the record groves. Tracking pressure is the amount of force or weight, measured in grams, in the vertical or horizontal direction that the stylus places on the record groove. The tone arms on turntables are usually more free to pivot than are those on record changers, but both should require considerably less force than one gram in each direction.

a. A computer-controlled direct drive turntable.

b. An automatic record changer with a built-in preamplifier.

Figure 6-6. Turntable and record changer.
(Courtesy of Radio Shack)

Antiskating

Most good turntables also have antiskating provisions. Skating denotes the inward force on the stylus caused by a turning record disc. The greater force on the inside edge of the record groove cause more wear on that edge of the groove. This force may cause the tone arm to move (skate) across the record. A properly balanced tone arm does not have skating tendencies because the antiskating control applies a counteracting force in the outward direction. This outward force is provided by either weights or springs and is usually adjustable to match the stylus.

PRINCIPLES OF DIGITAL AUDIO

One of the most recent advances in audio technology that has been responsible for the achievement of a higher degree of quality in sound recording and reproduction has come from the fields of digital electronics and optics.

Discrete Digital Sampling

Digital audio uses methods for recording, storing and reproducing music or voice that are very different from analog methods. Audio signals which represent voice or music are continuous functions of time. An analog waveform example is shown in *Figure 6-7a*. Notice that it is smooth and unbroken and has an infinite number of possible values. Digital audio signals are characterized by a sequence of *unique* pulses or digital numbers, each of which represents a particular value of the audio signal at a specific moment of time, as shown in *Figure 6-7b*. The processes used to *digitize* the analog signal are *sampling* and *quantization*. These processes are discussed in the following paragraphs.

Sampling and Sampling Rate

Sampling is just what the name implies. At a regular rate, the value of the analog signal is "looked at" and the value recorded. The points of sampling are shown in *Figure 6-7b*. The effective output from the sampling is shown in *Figure 6-7c*. The recorded analog value is then converted to a digital signal representing the analog value. This is called *analog-to-digital conversion*. The periodic sample which allows analog-to-digital conversion is the first step in the digitizing process. These samples are much like the frames of a motion picture, which are many discrete pictures and when shown back at the proper speed produce a continuous scene. It is similar with the electronic process.

It is natural to question at this point what happens between the samples? Have we lost some of the analog information between the samples? The answer to both questions is found in the *sampling theorem.*

The sampling theorem (called the Nyquist theorem) says that *if* the analog signal is band-limited, and *if* a certain minimum sampling rate is used, the original signal can be completely reconstructed from the samples. So, how often should we sample to accurately reproduce the analog signal? The sampling theorem shows that for an analog signal with a bandwidth of "f_a," a sampling rate of at least "2 times f_a" is required; that is, we must sample at twice the highest frequency to be able to reproduce the original signal accurately. Therefore, an audio signal with a bandwidth of 0–20 kHz requires a sampling rate of 40 kHz for proper digitizing of its full audio spectrum to reproduce accurately all of the components of the original signal

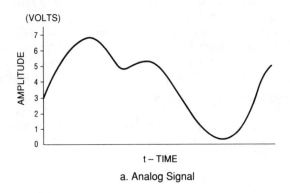

a. Analog Signal

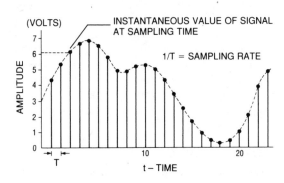

b. Sampling of Analog Signal

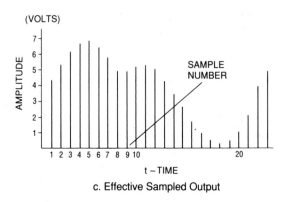

c. Effective Sampled Output

Figure 6-7. The sampling process to produce pulse amplitude modulation (PAM).

in the spectrum. Manufacturers have chosen a sampling rate of 44.1 kHz for the compact disc. This sampling rate is somewhat higher than the minimum sampling rate dictated by the sampling theorem. We'll explain the reason for this a little later.

Quantization

As shown in *Figure 6-7c*, the effective output of the sampling is a set of repetitive pulses. The amplitude of each pulse is the value of the analog signal at the specific sampling point. Thus, the original signal has been converted into a pulse amplitude modulated signal. The amplitude of the pulse is converted to a digital number in order to process and store the signal in a digital form and do all the number crunching and fast conversions that digital systems can do. The amplitude must be converted into a specific digital value out of a limited range of standard amplitude numbers called a quantum; that is why we call the process quantization. *Figure 6-8a* shows the quantization process using only 3 bits for simplicity.

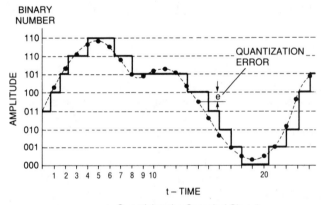

a. Quantizing the Sampled Signal

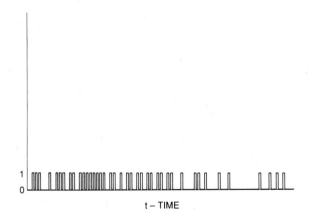

b. Pulse Code Modulated Waveform

Figure 6-8. The quantization process to produce pulse code modulation (PCM).

In *Figure 6-8b,* the quantized audio signal is converted into a three-bit binary word for each sample. The word length determines the number of quantizing increments available; that is, the number of bits we want to use to define each quantized increment. Since we are using binary digital numbers, the number of bits is determined by 2^n. Thus, an 8-bit word would provide 256 quantization increments, and a 16-bit word would provide 65,536 increments. As you probably recognize, the more bits, the more accurately the analog value is specified. However, no matter how many increments are available, the original analog signal may have varied between the sampling intervals; if so, an error would be generated.

Quantization Error

The difference between the actual analog value at the sample time and the nearest quantization value is called *quantization error.* At worst, the quantized value encoded will be no greater than one-half increment away from the actual analog value. The quantization error is related to signal-to-noise (S/N) ratio and the maximum number of quantization increments is related to dynamic range. Let's examine both relations.

Dynamic Range

As stated previously, if the quantization increments are 65,536 compared to 256, then the analog signal can be defined more accurately. In other words, it can be reproduced in more detail. Since dynamic range is the ability of a sound system to handle the softest signal to the loudest signal without distortion, we can see that the dynamic range in a digital audio system is related to the ability to define the signal in more detail. Therefore, a system with 65,536 quantization increments should have a much wider dynamic range than one with only 256 increments.

However, to have a good dynamic range, you must also have a good S/N ratio, so that the softest signals are not overshadowed by noise. The quantization error that we discussed can be described as noise. It has been determined—using the fact that the maximum quantization error is no greater than one-half the quantization increment—that the S/N ratio can be expressed in the following equation:

S/N ratio = 20 log (number of quantization increments)

As a result, *Table 6-1* gives the S/N ratios for 8-bit, 14-bit, and 16-bit increments.

Table 6-1. S/N Ratio for Various Quantums

Bits	Increments	S/N Ratio (dB)
8	256	54
14	16,384	90
16	65,536	102

The S/N ratio also is an indication of the dynamic range. The dynamic range for an audio amplifier should be at least 60 dB. If we use the S/N ratio as the dynamic range, then the 54 dB provided by the 8-bit (256 increment) system provides only a very crude system because the S/N ratio is too small and the dynamic range is too small.

On the other hand, in a live musical performance, the dynamic range of the loudest to softest sounds rarely exceeds 70 dB. From *Table 6-1*, we see that the system needs at least 14 bits to obtain an adequate S/N ratio and dynamic range. With 16 bits, the S/N ratio and dynamic range are 102 dB, which is 30 to 35 dB greater than the dynamic range needed. This means that when a recording engineer puts the 70 dB dynamic range at the top of the available 102 dB in a compact disc format (compact discs use a 16-bit system), and you set the lower reference (threshold) level of your playback dynamic range, you never hear the noise of the compact disc because it is at least 30 dB below the threshold of audibility.

Aliasing

Sampling is actually a modulation process and produces modulation products as we saw in Chapter 4. The spectrum for the sampled audio signal is shown in *Figure 6-9* for various sampling conditions. Notice that in *Figure 6-9b* the lower sideband extends down just to the upper end of the audio band f_a (20 KHz). This would require an audio filter with an infinitely sharp cutoff rate (which is impossible to attain) to recapture or reconstruct the original audio. This is why a sampling rate of 2 times f is never used. In *Figure 6-9c*, the sampling frequency f_s is greater than $2f_a$ (44.1 KHz); therefore, there is a guard band between the audio and the lower sideband. If the audio is not bandwidth limited, or if the sampling frequency is not sufficiently high, then the condition shown in *Figure 6-9d* occurs. The interference that the lower sideband produces in the band of audio frequencies is called *aliasing*. To prevent this interference, an anti-aliasing filter is used to prevent the audio frequencies from ever being greater than one-half the sampling frequency ($f_s/2$).

THE COMPACT DISC

Digital audio is such a big improvement over analog audio that anyone who hears it will have a hard time going back to traditional analog audio. Digitizing the audio signal eliminates most of the deterioration of the signal both in the recording and the playback process as well as the physical wear and other mechanical restrictions. Within the realm of digital audio technology, perhaps the most remarkable development has been the compact disc.

The CD system contains several technological features that are combined to form an unprecedented sound reproduction system. The compact disc has a track of microscopic indentations called *pits* as indicated in *Figure 4-9*. These pits and the spaces between the pits contain the digitally encoded audio signal which is read by a laser beam. They are embedded within the CD's substrate so that dust, smudges or fingerprints on the surface have little or no effect on the reproduced sound. There is no stylus touching the disc surface as there is in the phonograph, nor tape head touching the tape as there is in the magnetic tape player; therefore, no matter how many times the CD is played, there is no wear on the disc.

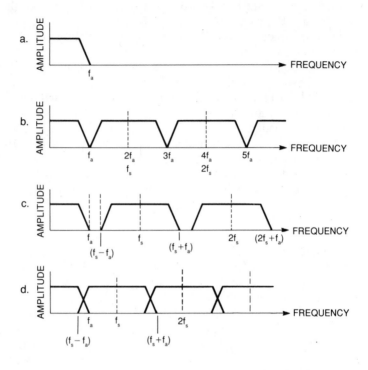

Figure 6-9. Sampling rates and antialiasing considerations.

Figure 6-10 shows how the pits are placed on the disc to store the digital code that represents the analog information that has been sampled. Note that the pits placed on the discs begin and end when a 1 appears in the digital code. The space within the pits, and between the end of one pit and the beginning of the next pit, represents the 0s in the code. The laser beam that reads the disc surface detects each transition at the edge of a pit as a 1 in the code; all other spaces are 0s.

The audio signal is encoded on the disc in the form of digital data by an elaborate coding scheme formatted prior to disc mastering. It is decoded each time the CD is played. *Figure 6-11* shows the format of one frame of the digital code ready to be recorded on the compact disc. Contained within each frame are 588 so-called "channel bits." For those of you who are interested in more detail, a fair amount of information is added to the original sampled analog signal. As shown in *Figure 6-11*, the 32-bit samples from the left and right channels are alternated as they are placed in the data bit stream. To the sampled data are added a subcode of eight bits used to identify program beginning and ending points, pre-emphasis points, total number of programs, etc., and a parity code using a total of 64 bits (placed at two 32-bit locations) used for error correction.

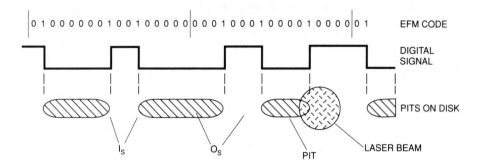

Figure 6-10. The compact disc storage of digital data.

This data stream, identified as thirty-three 8-bit data symbols, is put through an EFM (eight-to-fourteen) modulation process which converts each data symbol to a 17-bit code so it conforms to the 1-transition code scheme shown in *Figure 6-10*. As shown in the frame sequence of *Figure 6-11*, synchronization bits (27) are added to provide timing and synchronization of the coding and decoding processes. Since the sampling frequency of the compact disc is 44.1 kHz and there are 32 bits per sample, the data rate of just the analog data is 1.41 megabits per second; however, inclusion of the parity, synchronization and subcode bits raises the required data rate to 4.3 megabits per second.

The digital portion of the CD audio system is not stereophonic in the sense that there are two separate channels. We would have to call it sequential monaural. The single bit stream read from the disc by the laser pickup is truly serial (one channel) with time division multiplexing (time sharing) used to interlace the left and right channels of audio.

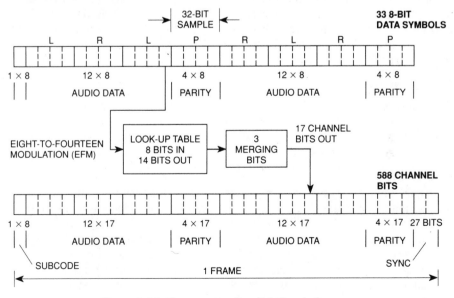

Figure 6-11. The compact disc digital code format.

7

SYSTEM
NOISE

WHAT IS NOISE?

Noise is any unwanted disturbance within an electrical or mechanical system which modifies the desired signal. To the listener of a sound system, this noise often manifests itself as static or hum. It may be a background noise or an occasional burst of static which is disruptive and annoying, or it may be of such amplitude and continuity that the program is obliterated. Any undesired signal that is present with the desired program signal, therefore, is classified as a noise signal. Although noise is commonly understood to be audible, in a wider sense it also covers visual disturbances in television and interference in data communications.

TYPES OF NOISE

First, we will classify noise into two general categories: *correlated* and *uncorrelated*. Correlated noise means that there is a relationship between the desired signal and the noise, whereas uncorrelated noise is present without the desired signal. Harmonic and intermodulation distortion are among the forms of correlated noise because they both produce undesired signals related to the desired signal. These forms of correlated noise were discussed in Chapter 3. In this chapter, we will concentrate on uncorrelated noise, which can be divided into two general categories: external noise and internal noise.

External Noise

All of the different categories of noise that arise outside of the electronic system are classified as external noise. The noise can enter the system only if the frequency of the noise falls into the bandpass of the system. External noise includes man-made noise, atmospheric noise and space noise.

Man-Made Noise

The most annoying type of external noise is usually man-made. Common sources of man-made noise include electrical power equipment—electric motor commutators, fluorescent lights, solid-state power controls, automotive ignition systems, and interference from radio transmitters, especially citizens band (CB) and amateur (ham), are prime examples. Most of these noise sources actually radiate or transmit their interfering signal through space to the electronic system receiving the interference. Sometimes the noise comes into the electronic system by means of the power line, and/or through the power supply of the system. This undesired noise signal will then add together with the desired signal in the system as shown in *Figure 7-1*.

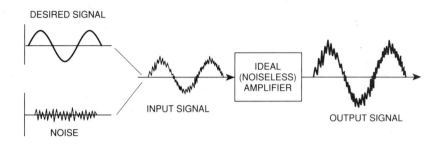

Figure 7-1. The effect of noise adding with a signal in an electronic system.

Atmospheric Noise

Naturally occurring disturbances in the earth's atmosphere—the most prominent of which are *lightning* discharges—produce static noise classified as atmospheric noise. This static electrical noise generally appears in the form of impulses which spreads its energy across a wide range of the frequency spectrum. Therefore, some of its energy will invariably fall within the bandpass of the electronic system and be added to the desired program signal. The magnitude or intensity of the static noise impulses from these natural electrical disturbances is inversely proportional to their frequency. This means that atmospheric noise is more troublesome at the lower frequencies, while at frequencies above 30 MHz, it is insignificant. Electrical storms throughout the world produce the largest quantity of atmospheric noise, but its intensity is greatest from nearby storms. It is most apparent when listening to a distant AM radio station at night.

Space Noise

Space noise, also called extraterrestrial noise, originates outside of the earth's atmosphere from basically two sources—our sun (solar noise) and other stars (cosmic or galactic noise). The solar noise is cyclical and reaches very strong peaks every eleven years with 1990 being a peak year. These eleven year peaks also follow a supercycle pattern, reaching a maximum intensity every 100 years or so. The 1957 peak was the highest in recorded history.

Distant stars in our galaxy and in other galaxies are also suns with very high temperatures, so they also radiate solar noise. Since the sources of this cosmic noise are much farther away, their individual effects are small, but they make up for it in their vast number and the additive effect of noise. This space noise is most noticeable at frequencies from about 10 MHz to about 2 GHz. Frequencies below about 20 MHz affect communications to satellites and space probes, but since these frequencies rarely penetrate the earth's atmosphere, they usually don't cause much interference with terrestrial communications.

Internal Noise

Electrical disturbances generated within the electronic system itself are called internal noise. There are several different categories of internally generated noise and some, such as *thermal noise* are also known by several different names.

Thermal noise is also referred to as *Johnson noise* because it was first thoroughly studied by J.B. Johnson in 1928. Its energy is spread equally throughout the frequency spectrum as is white light in optics; thus, it is sometimes referred to as *white noise*. Thermal noise is the result of random fluctuations of the charge carriers (electrons or holes) in any conductor (resistor or semiconductor). The noise is directly dependent on the physical temperature because the random motion of the charge carriers, which causes the noise, increases with temperature. The random motion is akin to that first observed by the English botanist, Robert Brown, as he viewed vibrating pollen under his microscope. This gives rise to two more names for this thermal noise: *Brownian noise* and *random noise*. Finally, because the intensity of the noise is proportional to the amount of resistance, it is also called *resistance noise*. Why is this important to the performance of audio systems?

All electronic components, including capacitors, inductors and semiconductor devices, generate thermal noise. As audio system amplifiers' gain is increased for more power output, the thermal noise voltages of the components adding together can become a significant signal to produce a hiss in high-gain amplifiers. Different types of resistors of the same ohmic value exhibit different noise voltages. For example, standard carbon composition resistors are the least expensive, but they generate the greatest thermal noise. The wire-wound resistor, which is the bulkiest and most expensive type, generates the lowest amount of thermal noise. Design engineers have found that a good compromise in cost and size versus noise performance is the metal-film resistor.

Engineers also found that they can express the thermal noise over a given bandwidth as equivalent to a resistance of a given value at a given temperature. For example, in *Figure 7-2* the circuit has a noise generating resistor that consists of a noise voltage generator, V_S, and a source resistance, R_S. Maximum noise power is transferred to the output load, R_L, if $R_L = R_S$ (maximum power transfer theorem). Therefore, you will see thermal noise specified as a given value of thermal noise generating resistance. With $R_L = R_S$ maximum desired signal is also transferred.

Noise Research

In his research, Johnson was able to show that the noise power is proportional to the temperature and the bandwidth which the system is able to pass. The power generated is given by the equation:

$$P = kTB$$

where:

P = average noise power (watts) in the bandwidth B
k = Boltzmann's constant = 1.38×10^{-23} joules/°K
T = temperature
B = bandwidth (hertz) of the device or system

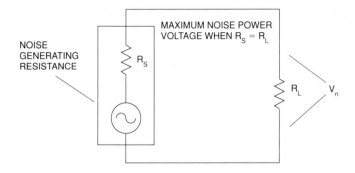

Figure 7-2. The equivalent circuit of a resistance noise source V_S showing its internal resistance R_S connected to a load resistance R_L.

Engineers have determined that if $R_L = R_S$ in *Figure 7-2*, then the noise voltage across R_L will be:

$$V_n = \sqrt{4R_SKTB} = 2\sqrt{R_SKTB}$$

Therefore, if an audio system (or a component) is measured to have a certain thermal noise voltage, V_n, at a given temperature and bandwidth, then this voltage can be expressed as a given noise generating resistance, R_S, by solving for R_S:

$$R_S = \frac{V_n^2}{4KTB}$$

SIGNAL-TO-NOISE RATIO

In measuring the quality of an electronic system, or in comparing one system with another, it is common to express the signal power P_s and the noise power P_n as a ratio. This power signal-to-noise ratio (S/N) is expressed in decibels (dB) as:

$$S/N \ (dB) = 10 \log P_s/P_n$$

The same performance can also be expressed as a voltage ratio by:

$$S/N \ (dB) = 20 \log V_s/V_n$$

The *noise factor* (F) of an electronic component, network, amplifier or any system may be defined as follows:

$$F = \frac{S/N \text{ power ratio at input}}{S/N \text{ power ratio at the output}}$$

When the noise factor is expressed in dB (that is, in logarithmic form), it is called *noise figure* (NF) and is one of the most useful figures-of-merit that indicates the degradation of the S/N as it passes through a particular system. It is defined by:

$$NF = 10 \log \frac{S_i/N_i}{S_o/N_o}$$

Figure 7-3 illustrates the meaning of the noise figure of an amplifier. When signal and noise are present at the input of an amplifier, each is amplified by the same amount. If the amplifier is *noiseless* (it generates no noise internally) as shown in *Figure 7-3a*, the S/N ratio is the same at the output as it is at the input. But practical amplifiers do have noise, and the one shown in *Figure 7-3b*, has internally generated noise of N_A equal to one milliwatt. This noise is added to the noise at the input (N_i)

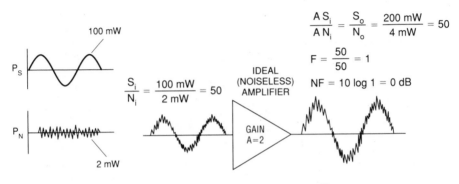

a. Noise Figure of an Ideal Noiseless Amplifier

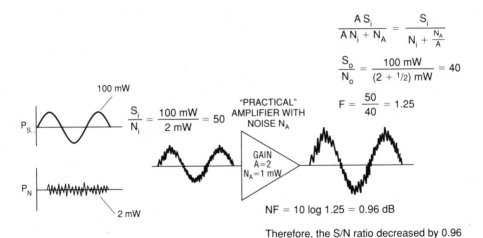

b. Noise Figure of an Practical Amplifier with Noise

Figure 7-3. The effect on S/N ratio by a noiseless amplifier and a practical amplifier.

amplified by the gain (A) of the amplifier. The total noise at the output is AN_i 1 N_A. The total signal at the output is AS_i, the input signal amplified by the amplifier gain. Therefore, the output S/N ratio (40) is less than the input S/N ratio (50). The S/N ratio decreased as the signal went through the practical amplifier.

NOISE REDUCTION SYSTEMS

Since high-gain amplifiers are used in audio recording and reproduction, noise can be a serious problem. With the increasing demand for quality sound, it is necessary to reduce the background noise level as much as possible, especially the hiss produced by magnetic recording tape. Noise reduction is essential with cassette recorders because the narrow track width and slow speed produce a higher noise level. Fortunately, noise reduction systems are available to reduce the noise added by the tape recorder. (Note, though, that these systems do not remove any noise in the original signal coming from the source.) Although several types of noise reduction systems have been developed, and companding was the original attempt, the Dolby™ and the dbx® systems are the most popular. Each has its advantages and disadvantages.

Dolby Noise Reduction Systems

Dolby revolutionized the reduction of noise in tape recording and playback systems. The essential difference between early companders and the Dolby system is that the Dolby system is frequency dependent. The compander was developed to reduce distortion and, thus, correlated noise. Dolby applies companding to frequency variations in addition to signal amplitude variations. Dolby adjusts gain as frequency changes. Several Dolby systems have been developed. The Dolby A and Dolby SR systems are used for professional recording in studios and are designed to meet those specialized needs. All of the Dolby systems operate on quiet passages, that is, low levels below about -10 VU. (VU stands for volume units, a measurement unit used by audio engineers.) High level signals do not need noise reduction since the program masks or covers the noise.

Home tape decks use either a Dolby B or Dolby C system. These systems are less expensive than the Dolby A and SR systems. Dolby B operates only at high frequencies and reduces tape hiss by about 10 dB. Dolby C works over a slightly wider frequency range and can provide noise reduction of up to 20 dB. Both systems operate during recording by amplifying the low-level, high-frequency portion of the program. The tape noise is not amplified because program amplification takes place in the Dolby circuit before the signal is put on tape. Very strong signals, such as over 60 dB, and frequencies below 500 Hz are not affected by the Dolby system because these signals are not degraded by tape noise.

When the recorded signal is played back, the Dolby circuit reduces the accentuated high-frequency signals so the frequency response of the record/playback system is flat. By reducing the high-frequency response, the high-frequency tape hiss is also reduced, hence the S/N improvement. To have a flat frequency response system, the tape has to be both recorded and played back on the same type of Dolby system. If a Dolby recorded tape is played back on a regular system, or with the Dolby system disabled, the high frequencies are accentuated. This gives the program a "bright" sound, which some listeners actually like. *Figure 7-4* shows a stereo cassette tape deck that has both Dolby B and Dolby C systems.

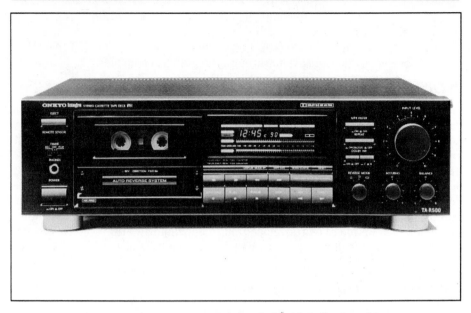

Figure 7-4. A stereo cassette tape deck with Dolby B and C.
(Courtesy of Onkyo)

The dbx Noise Reduction System

The dbx noise reduction system is a compressor/expander system that is connected into a recording system in the same way that a Dolby system is. It can provide up to 30 dB of noise reduction, but unlike Dolby, the dbx system works over the entire audio frequency range.

Dolby-encoded and dbx-encoded tapes are not compatible with each other. Systems using dbx noise reduction are typically more expensive than systems using Dolby.

Hum

Hum is one of the most common types of noise in equipment that operates from the commercial power line. Since the power line voltage is generated at a frequency of 60 Hz, 60 Hz hum is the usual problem. The 60 Hz signal is superimposed upon the program signal because of poor shielding or grounding of the program signal leads.

If the hum is added to the program signal by way of the power supply, it is probably due to a defective filter capacitor or voltage regulator in the power supply. After several years, filter capacitors lose their filtering ability and need replacement. If the power supply has a full-wave rectifier circuit, then the power supply hum will be at a frequency of 120 Hz instead of 60 Hz. Hum can usually be reduced by careful attention to the filtering and regulation of the power supply lines feeding the amplifier circuits.

8

AM/FM
TUNERS AND
RECEIVERS

A modern stereo system would not be complete if it did not include an AM/FM tuner or receiver. Using a tuner or total receiver, the user has an almost unlimited source of program material without having to bother with record discs, tapes or CDs. Originally, the AM and FM tuners were separate components, but because of several common circuits, they are almost always combined today to form an integrated AM/FM tuner. A tuner is different from a receiver in that it does not contain the audio section of the stereo system; it contains only an audio preamplifier. A stereo receiver, on the other hand, contains the tuner section as well as the audio amplifier section. We will first consider the operation of a tuner/receiver and then some basic theory of radio modulation principles.

THE BASIC TUNER

Stereo broadcasts on FM are common, but stereo on AM is new. Only recently have a few AM stations started broadcasting in stereo; however, because the audio frequency bandwidth is, or will be, 10 kHz, the fidelity is limited. On the other hand, almost all FM stations broadcast in stereo and transmit a full 15 kHz of audio bandwidth, which is enough for high fidelity. Tuners and receivers for both AM and FM are very similar, as we will see in the following discussion.

THE HETERODYNE PRINCIPLE

The basic circuit used in both the AM and FM tuners has remained virtually unchanged for about 60 years. It is the *superheterodyne* tuner. This name came from the word *heterodyne*, which means to combine or mix two frequencies together. *Figure 8-1* shows an example. It eliminated a whistle ("birdies") common in early radios. This is a very important basic concept: It is used over and over again in amplifier, receiver, transmitter, and tuner circuits. As shown, mixing a signal source with frequency f_1 with a signal source at frequency f_2 produces a new set of frequencies which are the *sum* and the *difference* of the original two frequencies. Any information contained on f_1 or f_2 as modulation is contained in the sum and difference frequencies. It is, in fact, the model for all tuners for AM, FM, amateur radio, CB, television, radar and satellite systems. We will examine the block diagrams for the AM and FM tuners individually. (Be aware that the purpose of all of these discussions is to help you understand the basic concepts and fundamental principles; not to make you a design engineer.)

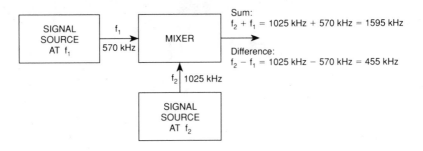

Figure 8-1. Heterodyning.

AM TUNER

The AM tuner block diagram is shown in *Figure 8-2*. Radio frequency (RF) signals broadcast by radio stations are picked up by the antenna, which is usually a ferrite core loopstick. Signals from the antenna are fed to the RF amplifier. The RF amplifier stage is a broad-tuned bandpass filter and amplifier with an *adjustable* center frequency that can be tuned by the user to the desired station's RF carrier. The RF amplifier circuit is used to select and amplify the relatively weak signal of a particular radio station. This signal needs to be amplified before it is sent to the mixer stage because it has the highest noise factor of all the tuner stages. Some receivers have more than one RF amplifier, and others have none. In strong signal areas it may be difficult to tell the difference, but in weak signal areas the receiver with more RF amplifiers will easily be the winner in performance.

Mixing

The output from the RF amplifier is coupled to the converter, which consists of the mixer and local oscillator (LO) stages. Referring to *Figure 8-1*, the output of the RF amplifier is the f_1 signal, and the output of the local oscillator is the f_2 signal. In this case, the local oscillator signal has no information on it. It is just a constant amplitude signal whose frequency is varied to give a constant difference frequency at the output of the mixer. The converter uses the heterodyne principal to convert any selected RF signal to one intermediate frequency (IF). For broadcast AM receivers, the IF frequency is the industry standard of 455 kHz. To obtain this IF frequency, the LO is operated at a frequency 455 kHz *above* the desired received signal. For example, suppose that the desired station is at a frequency of 570 kHz. To receive this station, the local oscillator in the converter would be set to generate a frequency of 1025 kHz (455 + 570). When this 1025 kHz signal is heterodyned with the desired station frequency of 570 kHz, the difference frequency of 455 kHz is produced. (Other frequencies also are produced, but they are rejected by the IF filters.) The IF signal contains all of the information in the original RF signal. As shown in *Figure 8-2*, the frequency of the local oscillator is changed at the same time the dial is tuned for a new station. This keeps the IF frequency constant.

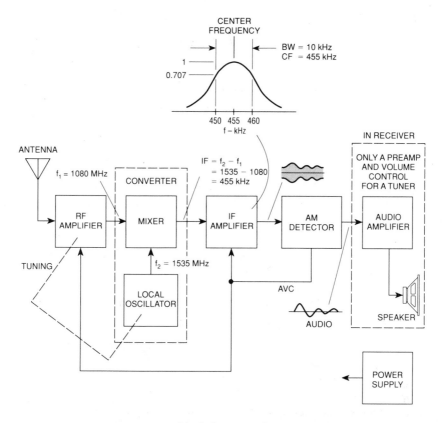

Figure 8-2. A block diagram of an AM tuner.

IF Amplifiers

The IF amplifier (which may be one, two or three stages) provides most of the receiver's gain and selectivity. An IF amplifier is not very different from an RF amplifier stage except that it operates at a fixed center frequency; that is, it is always tuned to the same IF frequency regardless of the frequency of the incoming radio station. In an ordinary AM broadcast receiver or tuner, the overall bandpass of the IF filters is about 10 kHz, which allows for high gain because of the gain-bandwidth product. The series of tuned IF amplifiers is commonly called the IF strip.

Detector

The next block in the AM tuner is the detector. As shown, its purpose is to convert the amplitude modulated IF signal back to the original audio signal. *Figure 8-3* shows a typical AM tuner or receiver IF amplifier, detector and automatic volume control (AVC) circuit. Detection of an AM signal requires a nonlinear electrical device—diode D_1 works great for this purpose. The output of the diode detector goes through a low-pass filter, R_1 and C_1, which passes the audio signal to the audio amplifier stages, while the higher frequency components (carrier and sidebands) are bypassed to ground.

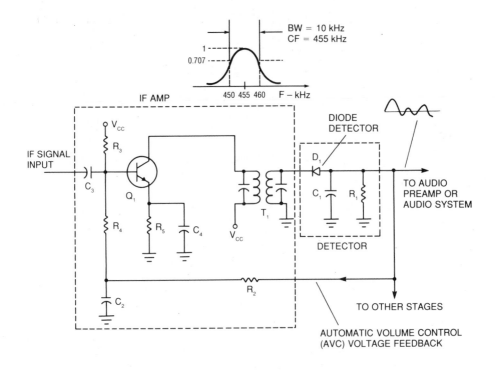

Figure 8-3. A circuit showing an AM IF amplifier, detector and AVC.

Automatic Volume Control

The AVC circuit, commonly called automatic gain control (AGC) with the introduction of TV and other electronics, increases the receiver's gain when it is tuned to weak stations and decreases the gain when it is tuned to strong stations. This helps to prevent weak stations from being passed over when tuning the dial and strong stations from blasting out the speakers or the ears of the listeners. Most AM radio receivers obtain the AVC voltage from the detector as shown in *Figure 8-3*. Here, the diode detector acts like a simple half-wave rectifier producing an average DC voltage that is proportional to the amplitude of the IF signal; that is, the strength of the received signal. Filtered by R_2 and C_2, this AVC voltage is used as a bias to vary the gain of one or more of the IF amplifiers and/or the RF amplifier. When the average level of the received signal increases, the amplitude of the AVC bias voltage increases, and the gain of the controlled stages decreases. When there is no received signal, there is minimum AVC bias voltage, and the amplifiers produce maximum gain.

From the detector, the audio signal goes to the audio amplifier. A receiver has a complete audio system, including volume and tone controls, drivers and power amplifier to drive the speakers, whereas a tuner may only have a preamplifier stage and maybe a volume (gain) control.

FM TUNER

Now, look at the block diagram of the FM tuner in *Figure 8-4*. It may strike you as quite amazing how closely it resembles the AM tuner of *Figure 8-2*. In fact, they are so similar, that we will point out only the major differences. These are the bandwidth and frequency of the IF amplifiers (and possibly the number of IF stages), the limiter stage, the de-emphasis network, automatic frequency control and the detector.

IF Amplifier

The IF amplifier strip is comprised of several high-gain wide-band amplifier stages with a fixed center frequency of 10.7 MHz and a bandwidth of 150 kHz. One or more of the amplifier stages are amplitude limiters which clip the peaks of the FM signal, thus eliminating the amplitude variations caused by noise or signal fluctuations (fading). To help improve the signal-to-noise (S/N) ratio of an FM broadcast signal, the broadcasting stations boost the high frequencies, which is called pre-emphasis. To compensate for this effect, the de-emphasis circuit in the receiver reduces the high frequencies proportionally so a flat frequency response curve can be produced.

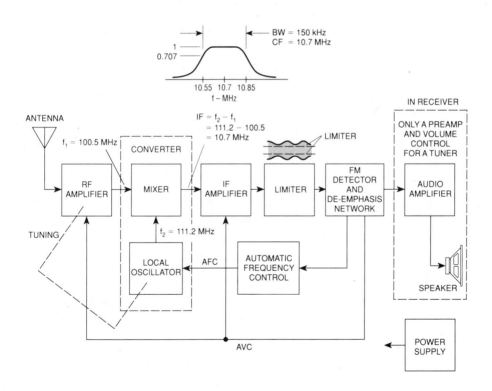

Figure 8-4. A block diagram of an FM tuner.

Automatic Frequency Control

Automatic frequency control (AFC) is used in FM receivers to prevent drift of the local oscillator (LO) so the tuner "locks onto" the desired station. Because the LO is running at a frequency of 100 MHz or more, a drift of just 0.1% could possibly move the tuning to the next station on the band. The AFC circuit is an application of negative feedback. It uses a varactor (variable capacitance) tuning diode in the LO. A dc voltage derived from the center frequency of the IF (which is related to the center frequency of the FM station) is applied to the varactor. A drift in the LO frequency produces a change in the dc voltage, which in turn, changes the reactance of the varactor, pulling the LO frequency back to the center of the IF. Modern FM tuners incorporate AFC into a digitized frequency-synthesized local oscillator using a phase-locked loop circuit (more about this later).

Detector

Where the AM detector converts amplitude variations into the audio signal, the FM detector converts frequency variations into the corresponding audio signal. The information for FM is contained in the frequency variations. Historically, there have been several FM detectors, including the *slope detector,* the *ratio detector,* the *Foster-Seeley phase discriminator,* the *quadrature detector* and the *phase-locked loop.* All of these types should have a response characteristic as seen in *Figure 8-5.* An output voltage, either positive or negative, is generated as the frequency varies around its center frequency. An example input and output are shown. Each of these detectors has experienced popularity in its time and place, but the phase-locked loop (PLL) has advantages that far outpace the others. Its small physical size alone (a small integrated circuit and a few additional components) makes it attractive to circuit designers, but its outstanding advantage is that it never needs alignment. These two advantages make the PLL the preferred FM detector circuit in commercial systems today.

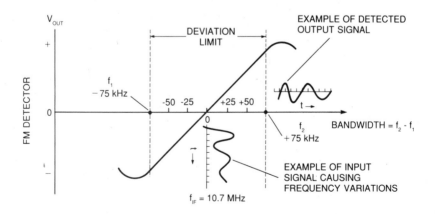

Figure 8-5. The response curve showing the characteristics of any of the FM detector circuits.

The Phase-Locked Loop

The phase-locked loop (PLL) has become increasingly popular in electronic systems in recent years. We will see it in several applications in this chapter and the next, so we will look at its operation in some detail. The PLL is a closed-loop electronic feedback system. Its basic operation is indicated by the block diagram in *Figure 8-6.*

There is a single input, V_{in}, and a single output, V_{out}, to the PLL circuit. The phase detector has two inputs: one is V_{in}, the input to the PLL, and the other is from the voltage controlled oscillator (VCO). The phase detector develops an output dc voltage that is determined by the frequencies and phase of the two inputs. The output of the phase detector is fed back through the low-pass filter and the amplifier to the VCO. The characteristics of the filter determine the frequency range over which the PLL will attain and hold its phase-lock, and how rapidly it will respond to input frequency changes. There are three possible states of operation for the PLL:

1. *Free-running* - The incoming signal and the VCO frequency are too far apart and the DC output "error voltage" of the phase detector causes the frequency of the VCO to change.
2. *Capture* - When the frequency of the VCO gets near enough to the incoming frequency, capture begins reducing the frequency difference between the two signals until they are the same.
3. *Phase-locked* - The input and VCO frequencies are synchronized and the error voltage is proportional to the phase difference of the two signals, keeping them locked together. The VCO frequency tracks the frequency of the input signal.

If the PLL input is a frequency modulated signal, then the output of the low-pass filter is the original signal because the output voltage varies as the frequency of the input varies. The PLL, when operated as an FM detector, requires no tuned circuits; therefore, it does not require alignment. It normally has high amplification which produces a strong output audio signal. Since it does not respond to amplitude variations, it also provides limiting action.

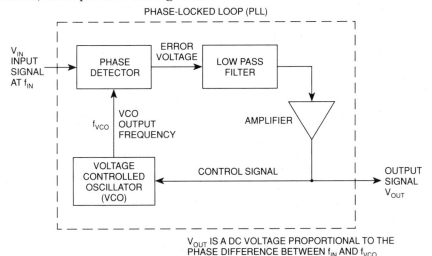

PHASE-LOCKED LOOP (PLL)

V_{OUT} IS A DC VOLTAGE PROPORTIONAL TO THE PHASE DIFFERENCE BETWEEN f_{IN} AND f_{VCO}

Figure 8-6. A block diagram of a phase-locked loop (PLL) system.

Since the VCO ends up at the frequency of the input signal, it can be set to tune for a given input signal. Therefore, many of the newer tuners and receivers now use a PLL in the converter section in the form of a frequency synthesizer to provide digital tuning. A picture of such a receiver is shown in *Figure 8-7*.

Figure 8-7. A modern AM/FM stereo receiver with digital synthesized tuning and a 55 watt, high-fidelity audio amplifier.
(Courtesy of Philips)

MODULATION CHARACTERISTICS

There are two fundamental properties of an RF carrier wave that may be modulated (varied) with the intelligence or audio: the *amplitude* and the *angle*. Angle modulation may further be divided into *frequency modulation* (FM) and *phase modulation* (PM). The end result of PM, for practical purposes, is FM, so we will deal only with FM. The AM and FM waves are shown in *Figure 8-8*. AM reception has generally been considered to be low fidelity because of several factors:

1. The audio frequency response is, or will be, limited to 10 kHz.
2. The S/N ratio is much lower for AM (typically 45 dB) so AM is more subject to noise than FM.
3. Harmonic distortion levels as high as 5% are permitted.

FM differs from AM in both the method of signal modulation and the quality of the resulting received audio signal. Some of the factors related to the FM quality are as follows:

1. The frequency response of the audio is limited to 15 kHz.
2. The S/N ratio is much higher for FM (typically 65 dB) so most noise can be clipped or limited from an FM signal.
3. Harmonic distortion levels are low, usually less than 0.3%.

Even with its poorer quality, AM is still a common part of even the finest audio system because of the large number of stations and the enormous programming choices of local and network news, weather, sports and "talk" shows. AM has served, and continues to serve, as a good program source for the small, low-fidelity portable radio.

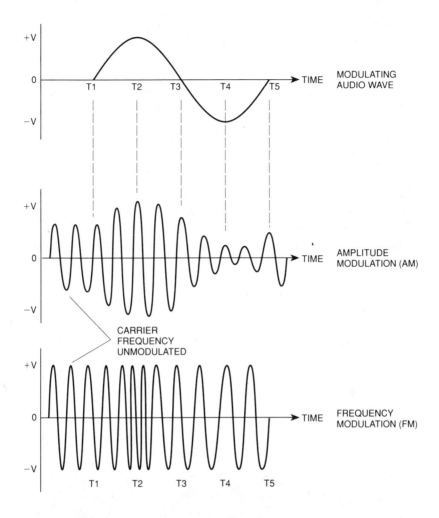

Figure 8-8. A comparison of an AM and an FM wave that is produced by the same audio signal.

ANTENNA SYSTEMS

Antennas play a very important part in the proper operation of your system for broadcast (through the air) signals. Pay close attention to using a proper antenna. The AM tuner for broadcast reception uses an internal ferrite-core loopstick antenna which is usually satisfactory. The FM tuner usually has some kind of internal antenna, but for improved FM reception (especially for stereo), a good external antenna system is important. Weak reception of the station will cause frequency drift, noise, buzzing, and especially a deterioration in the separation of the stereo channels.

Antenna Types

The VHF television channels are actually broken into two bands: from 54 MHz to 88 MHz (channels 2 – 6) and 174 MHz to 216 MHz (channels 7 – 13). The FM broadcast band is located from 88-108 MHz, between VHF television channels 6 and 7. Theoretically, this allows a VHF TV antenna to be used for FM reception in most cases. However, because channel 6 and the lower portion of the FM band are adjacent, they cannot easily be separated. For this reason, some TV antennas are designed with filters or traps to block the FM signals so they will not interfere with channel 6.

The folded dipole (*Figure 8-9a*) is the most common FM antenna. It can even be inexpensively fabricated by cutting a piece of standard 300-ohm twin lead-in to the proper length and shorting together the two wires at each end. Many TV antennas use a very directional antenna, called the Yagi. It uses a folded dipole as the active (driven) element with passive (parasitic) directors in front of, and reflectors behind, the active element. *Figure 8-9b* shows a picture of a Yagi antenna that is a combination antenna for both TV and FM. For more details on antennas and their installation, see *The Right Antenna* by A. Evans, published by Howard Sams & Company.

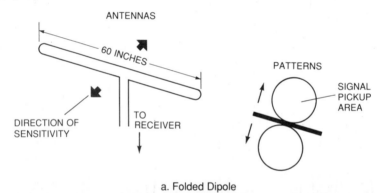

a. Folded Dipole

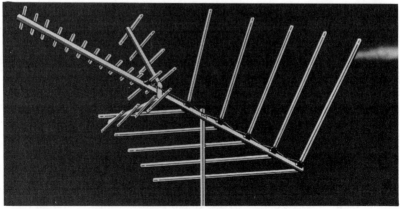

b. Combination Yagi for TV and FM
(Courtesy of Radio Shack)

Figure 8-9. Antennas used for FM reception.

THE STEREO SIGNAL

Stereo records and tapes became popular in the 1950s, and subsequently led to the development of a stereo FM broadcast method which was authorized by the FCC in 1961. A requirement of the system was that the stereo signal had to be compatible with the monaural receivers; that is, it had to sound correctly on a receiver that was not designed to produce stereo. The problem was solved by using *frequency division multiplexing*, which makes more efficient use of the 200 kHz bandwidth channel allotted to each FM broadcast station. Multiplex means to interleave or transmit two or more independent signals on a single channel.

FM Stereo Generation

Before the FCC approved the stereo system, it actually approved subcarrier transmission in 1955 under the Subsidiary Communications Authorization (SCA). It was usually used to broadcast commercial-free background music, paid for by subscription, for use in offices, shopping malls and supermarkets to supplement the revenue of the low-income-generating FM stations. The SCA signal is modulated on a 67 kHz subcarrier frequency as seen in the upper part of the composite signal of *Figure 8-10a.*

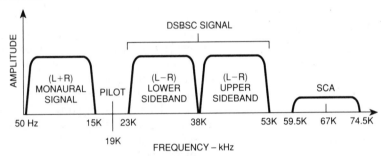

a. Composite Stereo Signal Spectrum

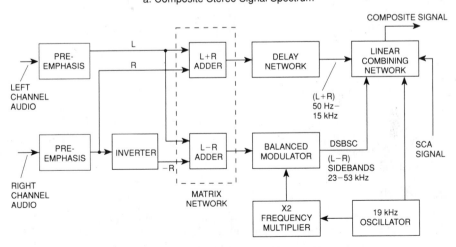

b. A Stereo Multiplex Portion of an FM Transmitter

Figure 8-10. FM Stereo.

The system for stereo (compatible with monaural) which was approved by the FCC combines the *left* (L) and *right* (R) audio sources in two ways, and then produces the composite stereo signal with a frequency spectrum as shown in *Figure 8-10a*. Remember that this spectrum shows the modulating frequencies, not the FM station carrier. The first signal on the lower end of the spectrum is the sum of the two audio channels (L+R). This produces the balanced monophonic signal and is assigned in the baseband from 50 Hz to 15 kHz in the spectrum shown in *Figure 8-10a*. The second is the difference of the two audio channels (L−R) produced by first inverting the R signal and then adding this −R with the L.

The process of generating a composite stereo signal for an FM broadcast transmitter is shown in *Figure 8-10b*. A 19 kHz master oscillator signal is transmitted as a *pilot* signal to be used in the receiver for demodulation to recover the stereo signal. This 19 kHz signal is also doubled to 38 kHz which is then used as a subcarrier for the balanced modulator. The output of the balanced modulator produces a double-sideband suppressed-carrier (DSBSC) signal assigned to the 23-53 kHz portion of the composite signal, also shown in *Figure 8-10a*. Because the (L−R) signal goes through a more involved process than the (L+R) signal, the (L+R) signal is given a slight delay so that they arrive at the FM modulator in the proper phase or time relationship.

FM Stereo Reception

The FM receiver block diagram shown in *Figure 8-11* details the stereo portion. Compare *Figure 8-11* to *Figure 8-4* and you can see that the stereo receiver's detector output contains the (L+R), the 19 kHz pilot (which is above the 15 kHz limit of the audio system), and the 23-53 kHz (L−R) DSBSC signal. The (L+R) is a full monophonic audio signal and is the signal that the audio portion of a monaural receiver processes. A stereo receiver, however, routes the three signals through filters to their respective portion of the stereo decoder, producing (L+R) and (L−R) signals. The matrix and de-emphasis network combines the (L+R) and the (L−R) signals to produce the left 2L and the right 2R individual channels (the 2 is only a doubling of the amplitude). A Dolby receiver would include dynamic de-emphasis as discussed in Chapter 7 rather than the passive 75 microsecond de-emphasis of a simpler receiver.

SPECIFICATIONS

We have thus far examined the various sections of the tuner or receiver and how they fit together to make the working system. Now it is time to see how the performance of the total system is measured and evaluated. Three major characteristic specifications of any tuner or receiver are its sensitivity, selectivity and S/N ratio. The S/N ratio was discussed in Chapter 7, and we will cover sensitivity and selectivity now.

Sensitivity

Sensitivity is the ability of a receiver to pick up and reproduce weak signals. It defines the *minimum* input signal at the antenna (in microvolts) that will result in a signal at the detector output terminals that is 20 dB above the noise (called 20 dB of "quieting"). Since different impedances affect this voltage value, a reference to a power level is becoming popular. The specification is given in dBf, which uses as

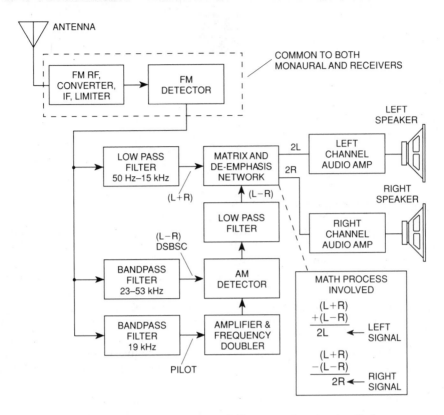

Figure 8-11. An FM receiver with the stereo decoder detailed.

a reference a power level of 1 femtowatt or 10^{-15} watt. The receiver shown in *Figure 8-7* has a sensitivity of 9.8 dBf. This is equivalent to 1.7 microvolts at the antenna across a receiver input impedance of 300 ohms. The 9.8 dBf is equivalent to 0.85 microvolts when the receiver input impedance, Z_{IN}, is 72 ohms, and 3.09 microvolts when Z_{IN} is 1,000 ohms.

Selectivity

Selectivity is the receivers ability to accept a given band of frequencies at its input while rejecting all others. It is usually stated as a decrease in response (in dB) at specified deviations from the tuned center frequency. The receiver shown in *Figure 8-7* has a selectivity of 60 dB over adjacent channels. Selectivity is related to image rejection, a potential problem inherent in superheterodyne receivers. The image rejection in this receiver is 75 dB.

SUMMARY

The functions that have advanced the most in the last decade are automatic tuning and storage of station frequencies. Phase-locked loops, digital tuning, and solid-state memory have contributed to the advancement, causing increased acceptance of radio by the consumer. These same techniques are applied to video and TV stereo systems discussed in the next chapter.

9

Video
and
TV Stereo

INTRODUCTION

Television dominates the home-entertainment industry, and for its half-century lifetime, the reception of broadcast channels has been its major emphasis. However, new concepts and components have been introduced, especially in the past decade, which have broadened the scope of home-entertainment video. First, the home videotape cassette recorder (VCR) has become extremely popular for both recording off-the-air broadcasts for viewing at a more convenient time and for playing commercially prerecorded movies and other programs. The VCR has prompted the development of the small home TV camera and the combination camera-VCR called the camcorder. Second, a large amount of video programming is now distributed over cable systems directly into homes and businesses without reception by antenna. Third, satellite transmissions and reception have brought video programming into the remotest areas of the country.

TELEVISION SYSTEMS

There are two distinct types of signals needed for a TV picture. The first is that associated with the picture on the screen (video), and the second is the sound (or audio). Both are equally important to what we know as television. Simplified block diagrams of a television transmitter and a television receiver are shown in *Figure 9-1*. Note that the systems are divided into video, sound, and synchronization and scanning circuits. A television station is assigned to operate on a particular channel in either the VHF band (channels 2-13) occupying space in the frequency spectrum from 54 to 216 MHz or the UHF band (channels 14-83) which extends from 470 to 890 MHz. Frequency allocations of the channels are in ascending sequence and are contiguous except for a few gaps where some frequencies were previously assigned to other services. Each TV channel occupies a bandwidth of 6 MHz of the spectrum in which both the picture and sound information are transmitted. *Figure 9-2* shows the distribution of the signal frequencies over the 6 MHz bandwidth. Note the position of the video carrier, the chroma (color) carrier and the sound carrier.

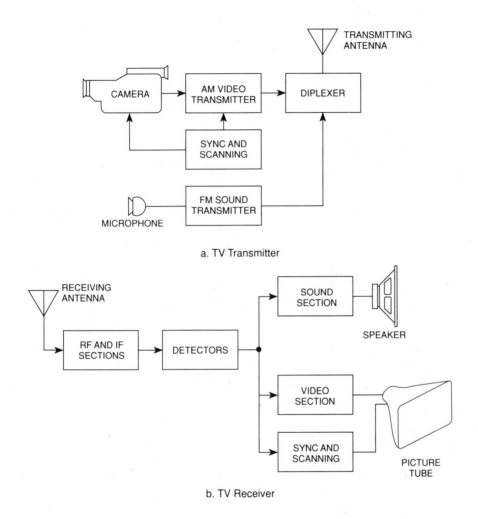

Figure 9-1. Simplified TV block diagrams.

Video

As shown in *Figure 9-1a*, the video of a television program is transmitted by amplitude modulation (AM). AM produces sidebands above and below the carrier based on the video information modulating the signal. Television uses a form of single-sideband transmission called *vestigial sideband*. All of the upper sideband is transmitted, but only a portion of the lower sideband is transmitted because most of the lower sideband is suppressed at the transmitter. *Figure 9-2* shows this principle for VHF channel 5 according to the United States television transmission standards. Notice that the lower sideband is only 1.25 MHz wide, but the upper sideband is 4.2 MHz wide. The total video bandwidth is 5.45 MHz.

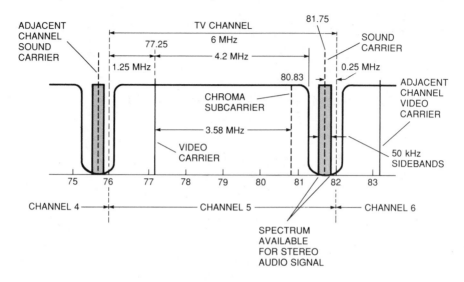

Figure 9-2. The spectrum of a VHF TV channel showing the principle of vestigial sideband transmission.

Audio

The audio of a television program is transmitted by frequency modulation (FM) (*Figure 9-1a*). In addition to the advantages of FM that were mentioned in Chapter 8, there is less chance of interference between the AM video signal and the FM sound signal. Television stations are permitted to frequency modulate up to a total swing of 50 kHz (± 25 kHz).

TV SOUND SYSTEMS

Monochrome and color TV receivers have a slightly different IF system. Color TV receivers have a separate IF strip for the sound, whereas monochrome receivers have a simpler intercarrier system.

Standard Intercarrier System

Monochrome TV receivers have two or three IF amplifiers that are common to both the video and the audio. These IF amplifiers pass the video IF and its sidebands as well as the sound IF and its sidebands. The gain of these IF amplifiers, as well as the tuner, is controlled by the automatic gain control (AGC) circuit. The function of the TV AGC circuit is identical to the radio AVC circuit described in Chapter 8, but the circuit itself is more complex. In the video detector, the video carrier is heterodyned with the sound carrier to produce the 4.5 MHz intercarrier sound IF frequency.

Figure 9-3 shows a monochrome TV receiver system with the intercarrier sound section expanded to show its similarity to a FM receiver. Compare this TV sound section with the FM radio receiver shown in *Figure 8-4*. Also, as described in Chapter 8 for FM radio, pre-emphasis is used in TV to improve the S/N ratio in transmission and de-emphasis is used at the receiver. The sound IF amplifiers are

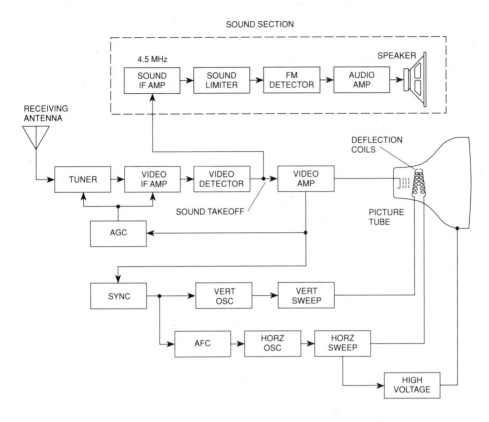

Figure 9-3. A monochrome TV receiver with the sound system expanded to show the similarity between the TV sound section and a FM radio receiver.

tuned to the center frequency of 4.5 MHz instead of the 10.7 MHz center frequency of an FM radio. The TV sound section has amplitude limiting to reduce noise and has an FM detector, just as does the FM radio receiver. After detection, the audio signals are amplified by the audio system to a level suitable for driving a loudspeaker.

In a monochrome TV, the sound IF signal may be taken off anywhere after the video detector; in most sets it is immediately after the detector. Some sets take off the sound IF after the video amplifier which means that fewer stages are required in the audio section. This sometimes creates a problem called intercarrier buzz or sync buzz which results from the sound signal not being completely separated from the video and sync signals.

Separate IF Amplifiers for Color Receivers

In a color TV receiver, as shown in *Figure 9-2*, there is a chroma subcarrier that carries color information. If the 4.5 MHz sound IF is permitted to heterodyne (also called "beating") with the 3.58 MHz color subcarrier, a 920 kHz interference pattern is produced on the screen of the picture tube. To minimize this problem, it is common practice to separate the sound ahead of the video detector as shown in

Figure 9-4. An extra detector stage for the sound strip produces the 4.5 MHz sound IF signal. Also notice in *Figure 9-4* that the video IF frequency band is from 41.25 MHz to 45.75 MHz.

Modern IF Amplifiers and Filters

Integrated circuits (ICs) are used extensively in television receivers and they form a complete section of the receiver in one device package. Outside of the IC, inductors and capacitors form interstage bandpass circuits and specific frequency traps, such as the 41.25 MHz trap in the video path that prevents sound interference in the picture.

Some television receivers use an entirely different method of filtering than inductors and capacitors. They use surface-acoustic wave (SAW) filters. The operation of a SAW device depends upon the piezoelectric effect mentioned in Chapter 4. A surface-acoustic wave filter (SAWF) is sometimes called a surface-wave integrated filter (SWIF). A SAWF is illustrated in *Figure 9-5*.

The signal to the input transducer electrodes is the television IF band of frequencies. This signal voltage causes acoustic waves to be set up in the substrate and these waves travel to the output transducer. Specific frequency and bandwidth characteristics are determined by the geometric configuration of the fingers of the

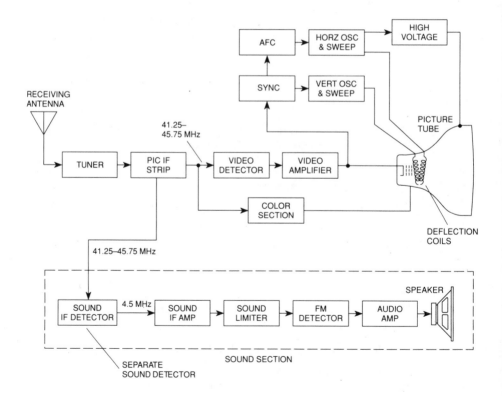

Figure 9-4. The sound system used in a color TV receiver showing the sound take-off before the video detector.

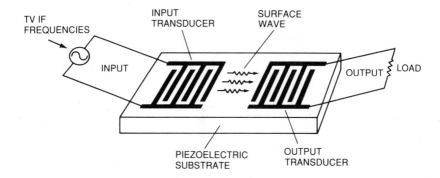

Figure 9-5. A surface-wave acoustic filter.

transducers. The SAWF provides the complete IF bandpass response for several modern TV receivers. Such surface acoustical filters are packaged in ceramic with an epoxy seal and they require no power supply voltage for their operation.

STEREO TELEVISION

Since the inception of television, the design and manufacturing energy of the industry has been focused on the production of a picture of the highest quality. Although effort is still under way to improve the picture, marketing has turned to a new and exciting addition to TV communications—stereo sound, and more.

The Evolution of Establishing a Stereo Sound Standard

As with the development of color TV, a requirement of a stereo television system was that an existing TV receiver must be able to produce normal monaural sound while receiving a stereo broadcast; that is, it had to be compatible. So, the design for a stereo TV system had to begin with the standard TV system. The first attempt to create stereo TV was through "Simulcast," where an FM radio station broadcasts the stereo sound and the TV station broadcasts the monaural sound and the picture. Although these broadcasts worked fine, they were terribly inefficient and impractical because they tied up both an FM radio station and a TV station for the same program. In 1979, the electronics industry began the development of stereo sound for TV. In 1984, the Federal Communications Commission (FCC) authorized the *multichannel TV sound* (MTS) system. The MTS system is not just the addition of stereo sound to standard TV, but a very flexible system that allows many different options.

Multichannel Television Sound

MTS is very similar to the FM stereo multiplex system that we discussed in Chapter 8. Since it worked so well for FM radio broadcasting, it required little change for TV stereo sound. *Figure 9-6* illustrates the modulating frequency scale showing the L+R, L−R, and second audio program (SAP) frequency positioning on the scale. *Table 9-1* compares the television MTS system frequency distribution and subcarrier frequencies to the FM stereo case we discussed in Chapter 8.

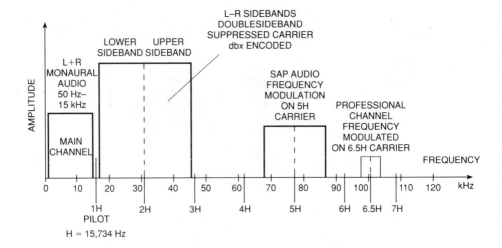

Figure 9-6. Modulating frequency scale for TV MTS stereo.

The experience in color TV with the 920 kHz interference pattern that we discussed earlier helped designers eliminate some problems in the MTS system from the start. To prevent picture interference, the pilot carrier frequency and the stereo subcarrier frequency were selected as multiples of the color horizontal line frequency (H = 15,734.266 Hz), as is shown in *Figure 9-6* and *Table 9-1*. The subcarrier for L−R is at 2H and for SAP at 5H.

Table 9-1. Comparing FM stereo to MTS.

FM Stereo Radio	Multichannel Television Sound (MTS)
Main channel audio (L−R) (50 Hz–15 kHz)	Main channel audio (L+R) (50 Hz–15 kHz)
Stereo subchannel (L−R) (23–53 kHz)	Stereo subchannel (L−R) (16,468.5–46,468.5 kHz)
Synchronizing Pilot (19 kHz)	Synchronizing Pilot (15.734 kHz or 1H)
Stereo subcarrier (38 kHz)	Stereo subcarrier (31.468 kHz or 2H)
Subsidiary Communications Authorization (SCA) subcarrier (67 kHz)	Second Audio Program (SAP) subcarrier (78.671 kHz or 5H)

Preventing this problem introduced another. The use of 2H and 5H subcarriers is a major source of noise in the MTS system. Pre-emphasis is used on the monaural (L+R) channel; however, the noise increases 3 dB per octave at the stereo subcarrier (2H) and 9 dB per octave at the SAP channel (5H). This noise has been reduced by increasing the (L−R) modulation level over the (L+R) level and using a dbx noise reduction circuit as described in Chapter 7.

A fourth channel, called the "professional channel," can optionally be used for communications between TV stations or between a TV station and its remote units.

At the transmitter, the left and right audio channels are matrixed (or mathematically mixed) just as in FM radio to produce the (L+R) and (L−R) signals. The (L+R) signal is transmitted as the main channel audio signal and standard monaural TVs receive this in the same way as they have all along. The (L−R) signal, again as in FM radio, is amplitude-modulated in a balanced modulator to produce a double-sideband suppressed-carrier (DSBSC) signal as the first subchannel. The second subchannel is used for the *second audio program* (SAP). The SAP subchannel is often used for second-language programming.

Figure 9-7 shows a TV MTS stereo receiver. It basically is the same as the FM stereo receiver that was discussed in Chapter 8 except the subcarrier bandpass filters are different and the pilot frequency is different. The dbx noise reduction circuit is included in the (L−R) signal path. Of course, the FM signal comes through the video IF and then the sound IF to the sound detector. The transmitter is very similiar to the one in *Figure 8-10b,* except the frequencies match those in *Figure 9-7* and special dbx noise encoders are added.

The TV FM sound system had the inherent capability of reproducing high-fidelity audio (50 Hz to 15 kHz) all along, though receiver manufacturers have not taken advantage of this in the past; that is, the TV receiver's sound system has been generally quite poor. Some of the more recent television receivers are being produced with an audio system of much higher quality. They have a built in stereo system, including a stereo amplifier and speakers, and the capability to receive both MTS and the SAP. However, to complete the system, broadcasters must transmit the signals.

SOUND ON A VIDEO CASSETTE RECORDER

Most VCRs are monaural and the audio signals are recorded on a standard one millimeter wide audio track at the top edge of the magnetic tape in the cassette. The system uses a separate audio head and the technique is much like that described in Chapter 6. There are, however, some differences that limit the quality of the recording. First, the narrow track is insufficient for even high fidelity monaural, and if it is divided for stereo channels with a guard track in between, then the frequency response, dynamic range and S/N ratio suffer drastically. The other reason for the poor quality is the slow tape speed which is about 1.8 inches per second for the fastest speed and only 0.6 inches per second at the slowest.

Both the Beta and the VHS format VCRs have a stereo "hi-fi" line, and both make use of the wider video portion of the tape for the audio signal. The Beta VCRs use the existing rotating video heads to record the audio signal. The VHS method of achieving high fidelity stereo audio is to add a pair of audio heads on the same drum as the video heads. The audio heads are used to record and playback the audio. These stereo hi-fi VCRs, both Beta and VHS, also have the standard linear track heads so that older tapes recorded on monaural VCRs can still be played.

This concludes the discussion of the electronics that are used to produce sound. We hope that we have covered the subjects that are of interest to the beginner as well as the experienced audiophile. We hope that we have contributed significantly to your understanding of the basic concepts and fundamentals, and that you will be able to apply them to your needs in the very near future.

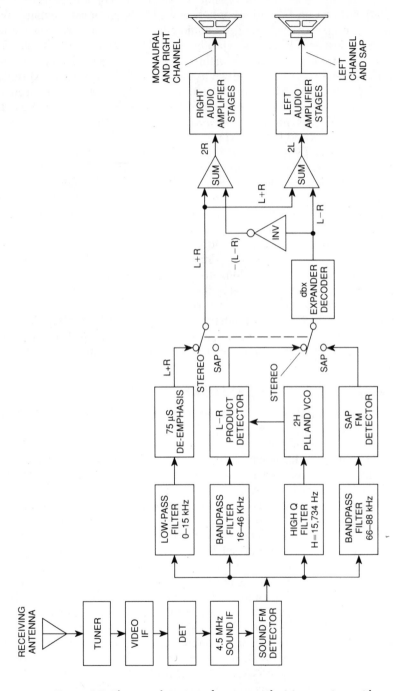

Figure 9-7. The sound section of a stereo television receiver with MTS and SAP capabilities.

APPENDIX

A. Logarithms

EXPONENTS

A logarithm (log) is the exponent (or power) to which a given number, called the base, must be raised to equal the quantity. For example:

Since $10^2 = 100$, then the log of 100 to the base 10 is equal to 2, or $\log_{10} 100 = 2$

Since $10^3 = 1000$, then the log of 1000 to the base 10 is equal to 3, or $\log_{10} 1000 = 3$

BASES

There are three popular bases in use—10, 2 and ϵ. Logarithms to the base 10 are called common logarithms (log). Logarithms in base ϵ are called natural logarithms (ln).

Logarithms to the base 2 are used extensively in digital electronics.

Logarithms to the base ϵ (approximately 2.71828...) are quite frequently used in mathematics, science and technology. Here are examples:

Base 10

$\log_{10} 2 = 0.301$ is $10^{0.301} = 2$

$\log_{10} 200 = 2.301$ is $10^{2.301} = 200$

Base 2

$\log_2 8 = 3$ is $2^3 = 8$

$\log_2 256 = 8$ is $2^8 = 256$

Base ϵ

$\ln_\epsilon 2.71828 = 1$ is $\epsilon^1 = 2.71828$

$\ln_\epsilon 7.38905 = 2$ is $\epsilon^2 = 7.38905$

RULES OF EXPONENTS

Since a logarithm is an exponent, the rules of exponents apply to logarithms:

$\log (M \times N) = (\log M) + (\log N)$

$\log (M/N) = (\log M) - (\log N)$

$\log M^N = N \log M$

B. Decibels

The bel is a logarithmic unit used to indicate a ratio of two power levels (sound, noise or signal voltage, microwaves). It is named in honor of Alexander Graham Bell (1847-1922) whose research accomplishments in sound were monumental. A 1 bel change in strength represents a change of ten times the power ratio. In normal practice, the bel is a rather large unit, so the decibel (dB), which is 1/10 of a bel, is commonly used.

Number of dB = 10 log P2/P1

A 1 dB increase is an increase of 1.258 times the power ratio, or 1 db = 10 log 1.258.

A 10 dB increase is an increase of 10 times the power ratio, or 10 db = 10 log 10.

Other examples are:

3 dB = 2 times the power ratio

20 dB = 100 times the power ratio

−30 dB = 0.001 times the power ratio

It is essential to remember that the decibel is *not* an absolute quantity. It merely represents a change in power level relative to the level at some different time or place. It is meaningless to say that a given amplifier has an output of so many dB unless that output is referred to a specific power level. If we know the value of the input power, then the *ratio* of the output power to the specific input power (called power gain) may be expressed in dB.

If a standard reference level is used, then *absolute power* may be expressed in dB *relative* to that standard reference. The commonly used reference level is one milliwatt. Power referenced to this level is expressed in dBm. Here are power ratios and dBm ratios:

dB	Power Ratio	dBm	Power (mw)
1	1.258	1	1.258
3	2	3	2
10	10	10	10
20	100	20	100
−30	0.001	−30	0.001

GLOSSARY

aliasing: Distortion (extraneous signals) produced by sampling at a rate less than two times the frequency of the signal being sampled, also called "foldover."

ambience: A surround or concert-hall sound.

amplifier: An electrical circuit designed to increase the current, voltage or power of an applied signal.

amplitude: The magnitude of an electrical signal above or below some reference, often ground or zero; usually measured in volts or amperes.

automatic volume control: A self-acting circuit which maintains the output of a radio receiver or amplifier constant while the input signal varies. AGC for TV.

balanced line: A circuit utilizing two identical conductors operated so the voltages on each of them are equal in magnitude but opposite in polarity with respect to ground.

bias: A voltage or current applied to an active device (transistor, diode, etc.) to set the steady-state operating point of the circuit.

capstan: The shaft in a tape recorder which rotates against the tape pulling it through the machine at a constant speed.

companding: A combination of compressing and expanding processes often used in noise reduction systems to improve signal-to-noise ratio.

compression: An amplification system in which low-level signals are amplified with high gain and high-level signals with low gain.

correlated noise: Noise that is related to the desired signal.

crossover networks: A filter that separates by frequency and routes the output of an amplifier to its appropriate speaker.

crosstalk: The undesirable presence of signals from adjacent tracks of a recorded tape in a tape playback's output.

damping factor: A factor defined as the rated load divided by the amplifier output impedance.

decade: The interval between two quantities plotted along an axis where the first quantity is ten times the second.

distortion: An undesirable change in a reproduced signal waveform that degrades the fidelity.

Dolby: A type of dynamic noise reduction system.

driver: 1. A power amplifier to increase the amplitude of a voltage, current or power signal; 2. any direct radiator speaker.

dynamic range: The range of volume from softest to loudest sounds expressed in dB which a system can reproduce without distortion.

echo: A reflected sound wave of sufficient amplitude and delay to make it distinct from the original sound.

enclosure: A housing for any electrical or electronic device; specifically used in this book for box enclosing speakers.

equalizer: An adjustable audio filter inserted in a circuit to change its frequency response.

fidelity: A measure of how well a circuit, amplifier, system or subsystem reproduces its input signal.

filter: A circuit element or group of components which passes signals of certain frequencies while blocking signals of other frequencies.

flutter: The frequency deviations produced by irregular motion of turntable or tape transport.

Fourier analysis: Finding the relative amounts of dc component, fundamental and various harmonics that may be present in a given waveform.

frequency: The number of complete cycles of a periodic waveform during one second, expressed as Hertz.

frequency distortion: The distortion produced when certain frequencies are amplified more or less than others.

frequency response: A plot of how a circuit or device responds to different frequencies.

fundamental or fundamental tone: The tone produced by the lowest frequency component of an audio or rf signal.

harmonics: A frequency that is a multiple of the fundamental sine wave frequency of a signal.

harmonic distortion: A deviation (usually undesirable) from the original signal caused by the presence of harmonic frequencies not in the original signal.

heterodyne: To mix two frequencies together producing the sum and difference of the two mixed frequencies; also called beat.

high fidelity: Refers to the reproduction of sound with little or no distortion; commonly called hi-fi.

hum: An unwanted low-frequency signal (usually at, or a multiple of, the ac power line frequency) present as noise in an audio amplifier system.

impedance (Z): The opposition (measured in ohms) of circuit elements to alternating current. The impedance includes both resistance and reactance.

infrasonic: Pertains to frequencies below the range of human hearing; formerly called subsonic.

intensity: The strength of a signal or the brilliance of a video image.

intermodulation distortion: Combinations of two or more frequencies which generate new frequencies which are sums and differences of the original signal.

loudness: A measure of the sensitivity of human hearing to the strength of sound.

microphone: A device that converts sound waves into electrical signals.

multichannel TV sound (MTS): A standard for transmitting stereo audio signals to home television sets.

multiplex: In communications, the technique of transmitting two or more signals over a single communications channel simultaneously.

Musical Instrument Digital Interface (MIDI): An electronic music industry standard for identifying musical tones with digital codes.

noise: Any unwanted signal or electromagnetic radiation, particularly that which distorts signals or disrupts normal operation.

noise factor/figure: For a given bandwidth, the ratio of total noise power ratio at the input to the noise power ratio at the output when the ratio is expresses in dB, it is noise figure.

octave: The logarithmic relation of sound frequencies used by musicians. The frequency of each higher octave is twice the preceding one.

period: For electronic circuits, the length of time required for one cycle of a periodic wave.

phase: The angular or time displacement between the voltage and current in an ac circuit.

phase distortion: The distortion which occurs when one frequency component of a complex input signal takes longer to pass through an amplifier or system than another frequency.

phase-locked loop (PLL): A closed-loop electronic circuit that automatically adjusts and locks the frequency of an oscillator to the correct frequency for receiving a signal.

piezoelectric: A crystal property which causes a voltage to be developed across the crystal when mechanical stress is applied; or mechanical movement is produced when a voltage is applied.

pilot: In a transmission system, a single frequency transmitted to control the reception process at the receiver.

pitch: How a tone sounds to the human ear. It is a subjective term because the perception of frequency varies with sound intensity.

potentiometer: A variable resistance with a wiper mounted on a rotating shaft.

power (P): The rate at which energy is used (voltage times current).

quantization: The process whereby the range of values of a wave is divided into a finite number of subranges, each represented by an assigned value.

quiescent: In electrical and electronic systems, the no-signal or steady state of a device or circuit.

reverberation: The reflection of sound waves from various surfaces so that "new" sound sources are added to the original.

rumble: A low-frequency mechanical vibration in a turntable or tape transport.

sampling theorem: A theorem which states that the sampling rate must be twice the highest frequency component in the signal being sampled; also called Nyquist theorem.

second audio program (SAP): A sub-channel used in multichannel television sound, often for second language programming.

selectivity: The characteristic that describes the ability of a tuned circuit or a receiver to select the signal frequencies desired and reject the ones not desired.

sensitivity: A measure of the ability of a receiver to amplify weak signals.

sound: The vibratory energy of air particles. The signals of frequencies from 20 to 20 kHz that normally are detected by the human ear.

sound pressure level (SPL): The pressure of an acoustic wave stated in dB.

spectrum: The complete range of frequencies from the lowest to highest.

spectrum analyzer: A test instrument that shows the frequency distribution of the energy in a signal.

static: Random noise in a communications system receiver due to atmospheric or manmade electrical disturbances.

thermal noise: An electrical signal which has energy distributed uniformly throughout the spectrum. Also referred to as Johnson noise, white noise, random noise, Brownian noise and resistance noise.

timbre: A subjective term used for human hearing that gives a sound a particular identity. It is related to the spectrum of frequencies contained within the sound.

total harmonic distortion (THD): The percentage of harmonically produced frequencies compared to a pure input signal.

transducer: A device which converts nonelectrical energy into an electrical signal or vice versa.

transient intermodulation distortion: A distortion which occurs principally during loud, high-frequency music passages in solid-state amplifiers that use large amounts of negative feedback.

tuner: The part of a radio or TV receiver containing the rf amplifier, mixer and local oscillator that selects the desired signal.

ultrasonic: Frequencies above the human hearing range; generally, the frequencies from 20 kHz to 100 kHz.

unbalanced lines: Any transmission line in which the two conductors are at different potentials with respect to ground.

vestigial sideband: In AM, whereby a portion of one sideband is suppressed.

wavelength: The distance a wave travels in the time required to complete one cycle.

wow: Audio distortion caused by speed variations in a turntable or tape recorder.

INDEX

BUSINESS REPLY MAIL

FIRST CLASS MAIL   PERMIT NO. 1317   INDIANAPOLIS IN

POSTAGE WILL BE PAID BY ADDRESSEE

HOWARD W. SAMS & COMPANY

2647 WATERFRONT PKY EAST DR

INDIANAPOLIS IN 46209-1418

☛ **Dear Reader:** *We'd like your views on the books we publish.*

PROMPT® Publications, an imprint of Howard W. Sams & Company, is dedicated to bringing you timely and authoritative documentation and information you can use.

You can help us in our continuing effort to meet your information needs. Please take a few moments to answer the questions below. Your answers will help us serve you better in the future.

1. Where do you usually buy books?_____

2. Where did you buy this book?_____

3. Was the information useful? _____

4. What did you like most about the book? _____

5. What did you like least?_____

6. Is there any other information you'd like included?_____

7. In what subject areas would you like us to publish more books?

   (Please check the boxes next to your fields of interest.)

      ❏ Amateur Radio   ❏ Computer Software

      ❏ Antique Radio and TV   ❏ Electronics Concepts/Theory

      ❏ Audio Equipment Repair   ❏ Electronics Projects/Hobbies

      ❏ Camcorder Repair   ❏ Home Appliance Repair

      ❏ Computer Hardware   ❏ TV Repair

      ❏ Computer Programming   ❏ VCR Repair

8. Are there other subjects not covered in the checklist that you'd like to see books about?

_____

_____

9. Comments _____

_____

_____

Name_____

Address_____

City_____ State/Zip_____

Occupation _____ Daytime Phone_____

Thanks for helping us make our books better for all of our readers. Please drop this postage-paid card in the nearest mailbox.

For more information about PROMPT®Publications, see your authorized Sams PHOTOFACT® distributor.
Or call 1-800-428-7267 and ask for Operator MP2.

 Imprint of Howard W. Sams & Company
2647 Waterfront Parkway East Drive, Indianapolis, IN
46214-2041

61026